Life in a
WEST GERMAN TOWN

ROBIN SAWERS, M.A.

HARRAP LONDON

This book is part of a series based on a concept developed by
D. L. ELLIS, author of *Life in a French Town*.

First published in Great Britain 1974
by GEORGE G. HARRAP & CO. LTD
182 High Holborn, London WC1V 7AX

Reprinted 1976; 1978 (*twice*); 1980 (*twice*)

ISBN 0 245-52423-1

Text set in 'Monophoto' Ehrhardt by London Filmsetters Limited.
Printed in England by McCorquodale (Newton) Ltd,
Newton-le-Willows, Lancashire.

Contents

About this book

You will not find Ritzenburg on any map of Germany. It is a purely imaginary town. On the other hand, it is very real to me, because it has so many features which are characteristic of places I know; I can really see it in my mind's eye. So although it does not exist, it certainly could exist.

In order to help you see it I have brought in an English boy, Roy Salter, who is spending several months in the town. You will also meet his young German friends who patiently answer his questions.

I have intentionally mixed the ways in which the information is presented. The first two sections are just description, setting the scene, but with the third one we move into some German homes and meet the people who live there. (From here on the main sections are self-contained and are not necessarily meant to follow one another in a particular sequence, so you can read them in a different order if you want to.) And so it goes on throughout the book – a mixture of straight description, Roy's experiences and dialogues. I hope this makes the book more lively and varied.

Ritzenburg from the north

1. History

Ritzenburg is a town in Central Germany on the River Bieler. It is situated in a narrow valley, near the point where the river leaves the tree-covered hills and flows out onto the plain. It started as a Germanic settlement at a place where there was a ferry across the river. When the Romans came they built a bridge. The first bridge was probably a simple wooden one; what is now called the Old Bridge *(Alte Brücke)* is a fine stone bridge built in the 16th century.

Merchants and other travellers going from north to south along the river or east to west across the river stopped here for the night. To start with there was only a small inn, but at the time when the famous missionary St. Boniface was bringing Christianity to Germany some monks founded a monastery *(Kloster)* near the river. This was in about 700 A.D.

Many years earlier, in about 50 A.D., the Romans had built a fort *(Kastell)* on a hill to the west of the river. It was part of a long line of fortifications called the *limes*, which protected the frontier of the Roman Empire.

Nearly 1000 years later, a knight named Johannes von Ritzen built a castle *(Burg)* lower down the hill. From here he could watch and control any ships on the river and travellers crossing the bridge. Protected by the castle as well as by its walls, the town became an important trading centre and its people grew rich. Then in the 17th century came the Thirty Years' War, and the monastery was destroyed by the Protestant army, who also damaged the castle. Both were rebuilt and added to in the 18th century in a very grand style called Baroque. The new part of the castle was called *das Schloß*, as it was a stately home rather than a fortress.

The town had been growing all the time of course, but it was in the middle of the 19th century with the coming of the railway that it started to spread out on the *Burg* side of the river. The station was built there, and a factory *(Fabrik)*. A wide street was built from the Old Bridge up to the castle with large stone buildings on either side. This new town soon became larger than the old town *(Altstadt)*.

Finally, in the last 50 years, the new town spread out onto the flat land to the south as far as the village of Hallbach, which it swallowed up completely. Here we find new housing estates with blocks of flats and also streets with smart modern detached houses.

A new and wider bridge *(Neue Brücke)* was built in 1900 to carry the trams across to the station from the old town. More recently a lock *(Schleuse)* has been built on the north side of the Old Bridge, so that barges can travel further up the river.

The present layout of the town can be seen from the following plan *(Stadtplan)*.

The 'J' and 'M' on the two churches refer to the Johanneskirche (p. 73) and Marienkirche (p. 74); *Brauerei*=brewery, without which no German town is complete! Page references: Fabrik, Schloß (5), Stadtwerke (31), Hbf (=Hauptbahnhof) (36), Stadtbibliothek (54), Tankstelle (41), Georg-Hann-Schule (43-7), Schwimmbad (48), Katharinenschule (44), Allgemeines Krankenhaus (66), Kaufhaus (18), Bank (70), Zum roten Adler (59), Postamt (68), Kino (53), Josefsspital (66), Spritzenhaus (65), Sportplatz, Schützenverein (49), Friedhof (73), Schrebergärten (16), Schleuse (5), Disco (53), Heimatmuseum (55), Theater (51), Schnitzelbank (61), Apotheke (19-20), Zum Löwen (63), Rathaus (28), Kloster (5), Marktplatz (25), Verkehrsamt (40), Polizeiwache (33), Amtsgericht (34), Bunsengymnasium (44), Stadtpark (48), Hermelinsaal (52), Jugendherberge (63), Hotel (62).

2. Streets

A town like Ritzenburg which has grown up over the centuries is a fascinating mixture of old and new. The earlier part of the town is quite different in character from the later part.

In the *Altstadt* (Old Town) the streets are narrow and winding, many of them still cobbled with *Pflastersteine*. These are oblong pieces of hard-wearing stone (usually basalt) about the size of a brick, but with a slightly curved top. So they do not give a perfectly smooth surface, which may have helped horses in the old days, but is no good for car tyres–they make a rippling noise as they pass over them and skid if they are wet. They do have the advantage that they can be taken up and put back over and over again (each time more unevenly), but the labour of relaying them is considerable.

The streets in the new part of the town are asphalted and straight, dividing the buildings up into blocks as we see from the plan. Some, like the Brückenstraße and the Hallbacher Landstraße, are very wide with trees on either side; they are rather like the boulevards in a French town. These streets also have cycle tracks between the pavement and the road. (This feature is more common in North Germany).

There are differences in the way the streets are named, too. In the old town the names often tell you what is (or was) found there (Marktstraße, Bäckerstraße), but in the newer parts they are usually called after famous people (Goethestraße, Bismarckplatz) or places (Breslauer Straße, for instance, which reminds people of a town which used to be German and is now in Poland).

In the centre of the main streets there are tramlines, except in some narrower streets in the Altstadt (such as the Hauptstraße) where the tramlines are at the side of the street. Like all the other traffic, the trams keep to the right, but they have the right of way.

Most pedestrian crossings are marked with black and white stripes *(Zebrastreifen)*. Many of them are at corners where there are traffic lights and are controlled by lights, with a green man showing when you can cross and a red man (or even two red men) when you must wait. It is an offence to cross when the red man is showing, and a policeman can make you pay an on-the-spot fine for doing so. Consequently German pedestrians obey the lights more than we do.

A set of traffic lights *(Verkehrsampel)* follows the same sequence as in this country, but is often painted grey. When it is attached to a building or hung over the street, it is very easy to miss the lights in the maze of tram and telephone wires, street lights, traffic signs, trees, etc.

Leaving the town along the Hallbacher Landstraße, you have what is called the *Grüne Welle* ('Green Wave'). This is a system of linked traffic lights. Beside the lights an additional light will tell you the speed at which you should travel to have green lights all the way; it says for instance "Grün bei 50". This speed (50 kilometres per hour) is in fact the limit within the town, and is equal to about 30 miles per hour. Since

Hurry! The red men are showing!   *'Grün bei 50'*

German drivers like to 'step on it' it is often exceeded on wide streets, but this is hardly possible in the old part of the town, where drivers have to be content with accelerating hard.

Parking, as you can imagine, is a great problem in Ritzenburg. There are a few meters in the wider streets, but where the streets are narrow cars are allowed to park half on the pavement, or if the pavement is really wide, with all four wheels on the pavement!

(Below) As in many German towns, one of the shopping streets has recently been turned into a pedestrian precinct. Can you tell what the German for this is? And when vans can deliver?

3. Houses and flats

A. Old houses

The great glory of the Altstadt are the *Fachwerkhäuser* (half-timbered houses). These are very old, dating from the 16th and 17th centuries. The wooden framework is usually painted brown with white or cream plaster in between. There are also some stone-built houses with beautifully decorated gables which are about the same age. Most of the later (18th century) houses are also stone-built, but with plastered walls and quite plain. They all have wooden shutters for their windows, and their rooms are small with low ceilings.

The few new houses fit in very well because they are in much the same style, with high, steep roofs and plastered walls. One reason for these steep roofs is to stop too much snow collecting (there are often quite heavy falls here). On some houses, a low metal fence along the bottom edge of the roof (called *der Schneefang*) prevents the snow from sliding off onto the heads of unsuspecting passers-by. Another reason for these high roofs is that the Germans believe in making the best possible use of roof space; every house has its *Dachboden* (attic) for storage, while many have rooms or even a complete flat *(Mansardenwohnung)* under the roof.

There is a big contrast on the other side of the bridge in the area between the river and the station. Here the houses are tall apartment buildings, rather massive and heavy-looking. They are all built of stone and date from the late 19th century. The rooms at the back often look out onto a central courtyard. The ceilings are very high and the rooms

Fachwerkhäuser in the Salzgasse

The 18th century part of the Schloß. The Schneefang is holding back the melting snow

large. The front doors are also big and impressive, often with glass in the top half protected by a grille.

The Krüger family live in one of these houses. They have the first floor flat. If I want to visit them, I first have to find the right bell *(die Klingel)* from the row on the left of the front door *(die Haustür)*. Having pressed it, I wait for a buzzing sound from the door which tells me there is somebody at home who has unlocked the door by pressing a button upstairs. This is a very useful device, which saves the occupants of the upstairs flats from having to come down to open the front door.

I press down the door handle and enter the dark hall. There is a light switch inside which I press. After a loud click a ticking sound starts, which may be a little alarming, but it is only the timing device for the light. It will go out automatically after a certain time (usually two minutes, so it is called *das Zweiminutenlicht)*. No wasting of electricity! If you have not reached your door and are nowhere near a light switch when it goes out, it is just too bad. However, courting couples have no objection!

The hall *(der Flur)* and staircase *(das Treppenhaus)* are rather cold and cheerless. The floor is of patterned tiles, the walls are painted brown up to shoulder height, and the stairs are of stone. When we reach the first landing, we find Frau Krüger waiting for us at the door of the flat *(die Wohnung)*. This is more like the front door of an old house in Britain, with a glass panel in the top half and a brass letter box and door knob.

Yes, Ursula is at home, so I am led into the hall which is again rather dark as it has no windows. It is really just a corridor with the other rooms opening off it. Frau Krüger takes me to the living room *(das Wohnzimmer)*. Ursula is sitting at the table doing her homework. It is

quite a big square room with a high ceiling. The furniture is a mixture of old and new; the sideboard *(die Anrichte)* is a very solid, heavy example of what is called *Stilmöbel*. It is made of dark oak, with rich carvings, and is about 100 years old. (However modern reproductions can be bought in the shops which look very similar). The couch, armchairs and coffee table on the other hand are modern, and the same as the Scandinavian teak furniture you see in so many British homes, except that the coffee table is larger.

The room is very hot (the central heating is extremely powerful), so Frau Krüger goes to the window to open it. This is a tall double one *(Doppelfenster)* ; the inner window opens inwards into the room and the outer one open outwards. In between the two windows there are numerous pot plants growing.

Ursula is very glad to see us and have a break from her homework. She suggests that we all go to see her friends Helmut and Lisa – their parents have a super new flat and a colour television.

We rush down the stairs together and catch the tram at the corner which takes us along the Hallbacher Landstraße. Here there are big detached houses in their own gardens, many surrounded with tall hedges. These are usually called *Villen* (the plural of *die Villa*). On the gates or on the wire fences are the plates with the name and (sometimes) the professions of their occupants: Dr. med. Heinz Ahrens, Arthur Meyer Zahnarzt (dentist), Wilhelm Gruber Steuerberater (tax adviser). This is where the wealthy professional people live and some of them have their practices. If you want to visit anyone in these houses you have to ring the bell at the locked gate, which is then opened from indoors if it is thought you look trustworthy. There may even be a small loudspeaker by the gate, through which a voice will ask you your name and business. There is also a box for letters and a tubular holder for the daily paper, so that the postman need not enter the garden. These people take no chances. And they say the *Englishman's* home is his castle!

B. A modern flat

We get off at the new estate *(Siedlung)* in Hallbach. This is a mixture of blocks of flats *(Wohnblocks)*, modern terraced houses *(Reihenhäuser)* and detached houses *(Einfamilienhäuser)*. Helmut and Lisa live in a block of flats which is only three storeys high. All the flats have balconies, and in contrast with the old buildings in the town, the walls are spotless white and there are big picture windows. Some of the flats are owner-occupied *(Eigentumswohnungen)*, while others are let *(Mietwohnungen)*. The few taller blocks contain council flats *(Sozialbauwohnungen)*.

At the front door we have the same performance of ringing the bell and waiting for the buzzing sound. This time we jump because Helmut's voice suddenly comes out of a grille by the door. Ursula says who we are, and he presses the button to release the door lock. I push open the door, which has a big frosted glass panel from top to bottom in a metal frame. The hallway and stairs are again brighter and more welcoming, with white walls and woodwork, although the floors still have stone tiles *(Fliesen)*.

Upstairs Helmut is waiting at the door to welcome us. "Hurry up, Roy! The big football match is just starting on television!"

Their modern flat is much the same as modern flats everywhere. The rooms are light, some with wide windows which are double glazed and pivot half way up each side, so that the bottom is pushed outside when they are opened and the top comes into the room. These are called *Schwingfenster*. The smaller and more usual kind opens in two ways: it can be opened on side hinges into the room if you want a wide opening

A   B

(picture A), or by pushing a bolt across at the bottom and releasing the top hinge it can be tilted so it is only open at the top (picture B). All the windows have net curtains.

As at the Krüger's flat there are many house plants in the sitting room, including an enormous rubber tree in a pot growing up and along the main window, which has many small plants on the sill. Outside the window is a balcony *(Balkon)*.

Inside, the furniture is modern and simple in design. The cushion covers, lampshades and curtains are in subdued neutral colours (what the Germans call "dezente Farben")–beige and cream for the most part. The room is very tidy and spotlessly clean. The parquet floor *(Parkettboden)* is highly polished and has a number of expensive Persian rugs *(Perserbrücken)* on it. These are liable to slide away under you, so you have to tread warily! Fitted carpets *(Spannteppiche, Teppichböden)* are found in more and more German homes, however.

The only bright colours come from the parasol *(der Sonnenschirm)* on the balcony and a modern painting on the wall–and the television, of course. After a time we get tired of watching the match which is heading for a goalless draw, so we go into the kitchen to see what we can find. Here there is a splendid array of labour-saving gadgets, including a dishwasher *(Spülmaschine)*, deep freeze *(Tiefkühltruhe)* and mixer *(Küchenmaschine)*.

"The new flats over there even have chutes for rubbish *(Müllschlucker)* which go down to containers in the basement", Lisa explains. "We still have to carry rubbish down to our dustbins."

We find some ice cream in the refrigerator *(der Kühlschrank)* and decide to mix ourselves a milk shake. Lisa plugs in the mixer, and I notice that it only has a small two-pin plug.

"Don't you have an earthed plug for a machine like that?" I ask. "This *is* earthed, silly," says Lisa. "It's what we call a Schukostecker. The earth contacts are in those notches. See?"

I examine the plug but can see no way of taking it off. "How do you get the plug off if you want to change it?" I ask. "You can't, it's moulded on, and there's never any need to change it because they're all the same, and every electrical appliance comes ready fitted with one."

The round socket is above floor level in the wall, and recessed. The power points all seem to be like this.

Helmut comes to see what we are doing, and says he wants some beer.

"You'll have to go down to the cellar," says Lisa. I look puzzled.

"How can you have a cellar with a first floor flat?"

"Every flat in the block has its own small cellar. It's very useful for storing things, and there's a washing machine for everyone to use down there too. It's in the part we call *die Waschküche*. The Hausmeister looks after it. He's the man who sees that everything is working properly in the flats, and that we are behaving ourselves."

"We don't have a caretaker, so we have to take turns at cleaning the staircase," says Ursula.

Manfred's Fertighaus

"But we do have a cellar. Most people here don't feel a house or a flat is complete without one. My cousin has a small *Fertighaus,* a prefabricated house – and even for that they dug a cellar."

"But aren't prefabs rather shoddy?"

"Oh no, not these ones. You'd never know they were prefabricated. And it was ready to move into only a week after the pieces arrived!"

"He seems to have a nice garden. Don't you miss having one living in a flat?"

"It's not too bad because there is so much greenery round here", said Helmut.

"It's different for us living right in the town," said Ursula, "but like a lot of our friends we have a garden outside the town which is called a *Schrebergarten.* We grow flowers and vegetables there, and there is a little wooden house where we keep garden chairs and tools. It's very pretty."

4. Shops and shopping

A. Introduction

Like so much else in the town, the Ritzenburg shops are a mixture of old and new. In the Altstadt they are small, mostly specialist shops with old-style shop windows, some with their old signs. One or two food shops have been modernized so that they now offer self-service *(Selbstbedienung)*. Their modern shop fronts fit in better than one might expect.

German shopkeepers often write their special offers with white marker pens on the window itself or with chalk on blackboards. They may even use little rhymes – Germans seem to be very fond of snappy little couplets, which are found in many advertisements.

There are fewer hoardings than in this country; instead posters are stuck onto curious round constructions called *Litfaßsäulen* which stand on the pavement.

A Fachwerkhaus with a modern shop front

A Litfaßsäule

In the new town and in Hallbach the shops are larger and more modern, self-service being more common in the food shops, and of course the rule in the supermarkets. A German supermarket *(der Supermarkt)* is much the same as a British one.

Just outside the town, there is an enormous supermarket called a *Großmarkt* which sells almost everything at greatly reduced prices. There are always hundreds of cars in its car park; people drive quite a long way to shop here because they can save so much.

The fresh meat counter at the Großmarkt

Supermarkets and larger shops stay open all day from 9 in the morning until 6.30 in the evening, but smaller shops still close from 12 to 2 or 1 to 3 at lunchtime. On Saturdays most shops close at 12.30 p.m. except on the first Saturday in the month (called "langer Samstag"), when they stay open in the afternoon.

B. Gift shopping

Christmas will soon be here, and the shops are full of good things. Frau Krüger and Ursula are going on a shopping spree *(Einkaufsbummel)*. I have been invited to go too. We start by going to a big department store *(Kaufhaus)* in the Burgstraße. Ursula thinks she will be able to get all her presents there, but her mother is doubtful.

As we enter the glass doors of this very modern building, we are met by a blast of hot air from overhead. We make straight for the escalator *(Rolltreppe)*. The layout is much the same as in big stores everywhere.

Only the notices are different, of course–*Sonderangebot* (Special Offer) is all over the place, while in one corner of the clothing department *(Kleiderabteilung)* we see *Aktion Wintersport* on a large banner; there is a big display of skiing clothes, skis and skates.

About half an hour later, we emerge with some wonderful bargains we had never intended to buy, but without having found just what we were looking for. "You get a better choice at the specialist shops *(Fachgeschäfte),*" says Frau Krüger.

So first we go to a china shop *(Porzellangeschäft)* where Ursula finds a cream jug to match her cousin Brigitte's Rosenthal coffee cups. Then we go to a splendid old tobacconist's shop *(Tabakwarengeschäft)* where the walls are lined with shelves and glass-fronted cabinets containing box after box of cigars *(Zigarren).* There is also a smaller section of shelves containing a wide selection of cigarettes, including American, French and British ones. I am amazed to find that the small cigars I want to send to my father cost only a few Pfennig more than the best cigarettes.

Next I want to go to a chemist to get some Eau de Cologne (or rather *Kölnisch Wasser)* but am not sure which sort of chemist to go to–*die Apotheke* or *die Drogerie*. "You want a Drogerie," says Frau Krüger.

The store's list of departments   *An old Apotheke*

"That's where they sell toilet articles, as well as films and that sort of thing. At an Apotheke you get medicines, pills, bandages and so on. The Drogerien are only allowed to sell medicines and tonics for which you don't need a prescription".

We go into a large Drogerie which reminds me of Boots, apart from the lack of medicines on sale.

Here is my conversation with the saleslady:

"Was darf's denn sein?"

"Ich möchte bitte Kölnisch Wasser", is my reply.

"Eine große Flasche zu sechs Mark zwanzig, oder eine kleine zu vier Mark?"

"Eine große und eine kleine bitte."

"Das macht zehn Mark zwanzig zusammen."

I give her a ten mark note and two 10 Pfennig pieces.

Next we visit a bookshop *(die Buchhandlung)* because Ursula has lost a school book for her English lessons so she has to buy a new one– and pay for it herself. There is a very good selection of paperbacks *(Taschenbücher)* so I buy myself some short stories by Heinrich Böll, one of the best-known living German authors. I ask for Christmas cards as well, but they do not have a large choice–it seems Germans do not send so many. They are either plain religious ones or views of Ritzenburg in the snow, many of them in the form of postcards (without envelopes). And no robins, holly or Father Christmases!

To end with, we go into a leather shop *(Lederwarengeschäft)*, because I have always heard that German leather goods are very good and not too expensive. This is quite true, but I am also very impressed by the attractive plastic materials, some of which (such as Skai) could easily be mistaken for leather. I particularly like Vistram which is very strong and has a matt finish, so I buy a red shopping bag for my mother made of it.

C. Food Shops

One general point: all food shops are spotlessly clean, and no dogs are allowed in, as this notice tells you.

Das Kolonialwarengeschäft: a grocer's shop where one originally bought foods from colonies overseas–rice, sugar, ginger and other spices for instance–which were called *Kolonialwaren*. This now means groceries generally. But there are not very many such shops left since most people now buy their groceries at supermarkets. In the righthand window of Herr Loman's shop there are bottles of wine and spirits, as well as beer and soft drinks. These can be sold to anyone at any time. Another drink sold here is milk, which comes in plastic bags or triangular waxed paper containers.

Herr Loman's Kolonialwarengeschäft

Die Fleischerei: butcher's shop. Just to be confusing, this is also called *die Metzgerei* in some parts of Germany. Here you can buy all sorts of meat as well as sausage *(Wurst)* but one notices that different kinds of meat are popular in Germany: there is a lot of veal and pork, and little or no lamb. There is about the same amount of beef, but the cuts are often different. One sometimes still sees a notice outside which says

EIGENE SCHLACHTEREI

This means the butcher has his own slaughterhouse, so that the meat should be really fresh. But what really distinguishes a German butcher's shop from an English one is the wonderful selection of *Wurst* (sausage). This is often made by the butcher himself, so it is very fresh. (The Germans insist on good quality meat and sausage, so this question of freshness is important).

Here are some of the best-known kinds. First those which are eaten cold in slices:

die Blutwurst: blood sausage. Made from pig's blood and pieces of fat. Like our black pudding.

die Mettwurst: a mild pork sausage.

die Bierwurst: sausage made from pork, flavoured with garlic and containing coriander seeds.

die Schinkenwurst: ham sausage.

die Salami: salami, type of smoked sausage with many spices, originally Italian. Keeps for a long time.

die Zervelatwurst: a fine smoked sausage, made from two thirds pork and one third beef and bacon. Keeps for quite a long time.

Next two which can be spread on slices of bread:

die Leberwurst: liver sausage. Made from pig's liver or calve's liver, either fine (like paste) or coarse, with lumps of liver and fat in it.

die Teewurst, 'tea sausage', a fine paste made from smoked meat; something like our potted meat only more salty.

Finally, three of the many types of sausage eaten hot:

die Bratwurst: large sausage for frying, usually made of pork.

das Frankfurter Würstchen: frankfurters are long thin sausages with a filling which should be mainly veal but now contains beef; heated by putting in water just off the boil for a few minutes; come in pairs.

die Knackwurst: short, fat sausage, usually with a smooth pork filling; heated like a frankfurter.

Das Delikatessengeschäft: delicatessen. If there is one in your town, you will know what sort of things they sell – special, tasty foods: cheeses, all forms of sausage, biscuits, special kinds of bread and so on. One in the Hauptstraße sells its own *Fleischsalat* (strips of sausage in mayonnaise), *Kartoffelsalat* (potato salad), and Liptauer (cream cheese with paprika and onion), as well as other types of salad in season.

Das Kaffeegeschäft: coffee shop. The Eduscho coffee shop in the Hauptstraße sells not only coffee and tea but biscuits, jam etc. The coffee is sold in the form of beans; this is called *Bohnenkaffee* to distinguish it from instant coffee. The man behind the counter will grind it for you if you want. He will ask you whether you want it coarse or finely ground *(grob oder fein gemahlen)*. But most Germans have their own coffee grinders, so they buy the beans, which are usually ready packed.

Many Germans drink a lot of strong coffee and worry about the effect on their hearts. They buy a special sort of coffee which has been decaffeinated, *i.e.* treated to make it less of a strain on the heart. This is called *coffeinfreier Kaffee* and the most popular brand is Kaffee Hag.

There are also jars of instant coffee *(Schnellkaffee* or *Pulverkaffee)*.

The tea is nearly always sold ready packed and the Germans prefer the milder blends, which they drink very weak.

Die Bäckerei: baker's shop. German bread comes in all sorts of shapes and sizes as well as shades – white, brown, grey and even black! Someone has counted as many as 250 varieties.

White bread *(Weißbrot)* is generally like French bread in long round loaves, but one can also get bread for toasting *(Toastbrot)* in square loaves, often ready cut. The various kinds of dark bread are quite different from ours in appearance and taste as they are mostly made of rye flour. The most common rye bread *(Roggenbrot)* is *Graubrot* ('grey bread') which comes in large oval-section loaves. It will keep quite a long time as it is more solid to start with than our bread with a thicker texture. This also makes it more filling. Its colour is a greyish brown and it has a taste of its own, sometimes made stronger by the addition of caraway seeds *(Kümmel)*. Then there is *Mischbrot* (mixed bread) which contains a mixture of rye flour and wheat flour, and *Vollkornbrot*, which is dark brown and made from whole grains (something like wholemeal).

One variety of this is black bread *(Schwarzbrot)*, another rye bread, of which the blackest and thickest version is the famous *Pumpernickel*. It usually comes wrapped in silver foil and ready sliced, being difficult to cut.

One can also of course buy various kinds of rolls *(Brötchen)*. A few bakers still deliver them early in the morning, so that one has really fresh rolls for breakfast.

All these varieties of bread (except for *Schwarzbrot*) are baked by the baker himself. However he does not usually sell cakes as well; for these you have to go to a *Konditorei*.

Die Konditorei: cake and confectionery shop. Very often, as in the case of the Café-Konditorei Döring in the Hauptstraße (see also p. 56), this is combined with a café where one can eat the cakes and drink coffee or tea on the premises. Nearly all *Konditoreien* bake their own cakes, and a splendid sight they are! Cream cakes are still the most popular, and these are usually very large; most people buy them by the slice. Ursula's favourite is the *Schwarzwälder Kirschtorte* (Black Forest cherry cake). This is a chocolate sponge with 3 layers of whipped cream filling, the bottom one containing black cherries soaked in alcohol. I prefer the fruit flans *(Obsttorten)* : sponge flan cases filled with fresh fruit such as strawberries *(Erdbeeren)*, raspberries *(Himbeeren)*, plums *(Pflaumen)* or small plums *(Zwetschen)* and usually served with lashings of whipped cream *(Schlagsahne)*.

(You may have learnt that the word for cake is *der Kuchen*, which is quite right; generally it is only where the cake part is sponge and its shape is round that it is called a *Torte)*.

There are plainer small cakes too, such as *Bienenstich* (literally 'bee sting') which has a sort of custard inside and almonds on top and *Berliner Pfannkuchen* ('Berlin pancakes') which are what we call doughnuts. But there is nothing which is really like our scones and teacakes, although the *Rosinenbrötchen* is a distant relation of a currant bun.

Das Fischgeschäft: fishmonger's shop. At Herr Kienzl's shop in the Johannesstraße one does not see very much cod or other fresh saltwater fish, although there is usually some *Goldbarsch* (redfish). On the other hand there are several kinds of freshwater fish from the river and from the streams which come down from the hills nearby. For instance near the door is a large tank full of live eels *(Aale)*, trout *(Forellen)* and carp *(Karpfen)*. You can choose which one you want and Herr Kienzl will fish it out for you in a net and knock it on the head to kill it. So it

could not be fresher! The eels *(Aale)* are eaten fresh or smoked *(geräuchert)*, but they can also be bought in aspic, while carp is regarded as a treat and eaten on special occasions (including Christmas).

Apart from tinned fish, the one sea fish which you will always find is pickled herring. It comes as a filleted strip often rolled up, which explains the odd name – *der Rollmops*.

Das Reformhaus: not a borstal, but a health food store, full of herbal remedies and special teas. They have peppermint tea *(Pfefferminztee)*, camomile tea *(Kamillentee)*, rose hip tea *(Hagebuttentee)*, and so on.

Die Obst- und Gemüsehandlung: greengrocer's. Fruit and especially vegetables are generally cheaper and fresher in the market, so let's go there instead.

D. Der Markt

Today is Wednesday and it is market day, so the *Marktplatz* (market place) in the Altstadt is transformed. Instead of rows of parked cars as on a normal day, there are rows of stalls, many with brightly coloured awnings almost hiding the fine old fountain *(Brunnen)*. In contrast, most of the countrywomen selling their fruit and vegetables are dressed in black. Vegetables common in Germany, but which you do not often find in Britain, are red cabbage *(Rotkohl* or *Rotkraut)* and red and green peppers *(rote und grüne Paprika)*. Tomatoes from the south sometimes look different too – they are much bigger and have ridges.

Fruits which are grown in South Germany include apricots *(Aprikosen)*, peaches *(Pfirsiche)* and grapes *(Trauben)*. All these can be bought from the market at the right time of the year. Some German varieties of apple are different from ours, such as the Boskop, which has a rough brownish skin.

Here Frau Krüger is buying a lettuce. What else can you see on the stall?

There are many other kinds of food you can buy at the market. The cheese stall can be smelt from quite a distance! That is mainly the fault of the sticky (and very strong) *Harzer Käse*. If you want something milder there's *Emmentaler* with the big holes in it, or *Tilsiter* with the smaller holes (it also makes a smaller hole in your pocket!) Another good smell comes from the far corner of the Marktplatz, where Frau Heinemann has her hot dog stall *(Würstchenstand)*. And who's that munching at a Frankfurter and a roll (with lashings of mustard of course)? It's the ever hungry Lisa!

If you want to buy sausages to take home there is a stall next door with a big notice saying *Wurstwaren*. You can get all the types of sausage mentioned on p. 22 here, and many more besides.

Of course you can buy many other things apart from food in the market. Flowers, for instance. We go to Frau Held's flower stall because Lisa wants to buy some for her mother and see this old lady there:

E. Das Kleidergeschäft

Fashions are becoming more and more international so that German clothes nowadays look much the same as English clothes. (Boutiques usually have English names for a start–'Miss London' for instance). One thing you will not find is school uniform, which is not worn; on the other hand you can still find leather shorts *(Lederhosen)* and the traditional huntsman's jackets and hats. The most important difference is the range of sizes both for clothes and shoes.

Men's sizes (Herrengrößen)
There are four different ranges:
1. Normal–42-58 (even numbers)
2. Short–24-28
3. Slim–90, 94, 98, 102
4. Outsize–51, 53, 55, 57

Each short size has the same chest measurements as the normal size you get by multiplying it by two: 24=48 and so on. With the outsizes 51=50, 53=52 etc.

There is a different range for underwear: 3-8.

Women's sizes (Damengrößen)
Here there are three ranges:

N (=normal) 36-60 (even numbers)
K (=short) 18-26
Ü (=outsize) 542-548

Again you double the short sizes to get the corresponding normal size; with the outsizes you just take away the 5.

Shoe sizes (Schuhgrößen)
The continental sizes 35-47 are being replaced by some firms with the English sizes $2\frac{1}{2}$-12.

English sizes	$2\frac{1}{2}$	3	$3\frac{1}{2}$	4	$4\frac{1}{2}$	5	$5\frac{1}{2}$	6	$6\frac{1}{2}$
German sizes		35		36		37		38		39		40

English sizes	7	$7\frac{1}{2}$	8	$8\frac{1}{2}$	9	$9\frac{1}{2}$	10	$10\frac{1}{2}$	11
German sizes		41		42		43		44		45		46

As you see, they do not correspond exactly. It is even more difficult to give equivalents for clothes sizes, so it is best to let yourself be measured.

5. Administration
or Who runs Ritzenburg?

A. Das Rathaus

The other day I was passing the beautiful *Rathaus* (town hall) on the Marktplatz with Helmut, so I asked him whether Ritzenburg has a mayor and who appointed him.

"Yes, Roy, and he is called the *Bürgermeister*, or *Oberbürgermeister* in a larger town. He's the head of the *Gemeinde* (that means community) and he gets elected by the town council for a period of eight years".

"That's a long time. We have elections more often than that".

"So do we—we have local elections every four years in fact to elect a new town council. It's only the mayor who goes on for eight years, or twelve if he's re-elected."

"You seem to know a lot about it."

"Yes, my father's on the town council – *Stadtrat* it's called."

"But I thought he had a flower shop."

"So he does, his work on the council is only part time. Only the Bürgermeister works full time."

"It must be difficult to run everything working only a few hours a week."

"Oh well, most of the routine administration is done by civil servants in the different offices. They're not elected of course, they have permanent jobs. You'll find a list of the offices in the entrance to the Rathaus. Some are in the same building, but most of them are in separate buildings because the old Rathaus is too small. You see, Ritzenburg is a *Kreisstadt*, so the administrative offices for the surrounding areas are all here."

"What is a Kreisstadt?"

"It's the chief town in a *Kreis*, which is an administrative district made up of several *Gemeinden*. Our *Land* is divided into about 60 *Kreise*. You know what a Land is, I hope?"

"Yes, it's something like an English county, except it's usually much bigger and has more independence. There are only ten of them, I think."

(Here is a diagram showing these three administrative units:

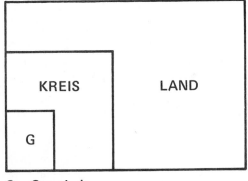

G = Gemeinde

Admittedly, it doesn't always work like this. Larger towns already count as *Kreise* which are then called *Stadtkreise*).

We then went into the Rathaus. Apart from the *Bürgermeisteramt* (Mayor's Office), there is only one *Amt* (Office) in the town hall itself: the *Ordnungsamt* (Public Order Office). It issues passports and identity cards and keeps records and photographs of all inhabitants of the town; when you move to Ritzenburg you have to report there, and even if you are only spending a few nights in a hotel or guest house you are supposed to fill in a small form giving all your personal details. You don't have to if you are staying with friends for three days or less, and people often do not bother even for longer stays. Here is a copy of such a form:

Für amtliche Vermerke

Meldeschein der Beherbergungsstätten

HOTEL

Kronenmüller

RITZENBURG

BRESLAUER STRAßE 5 Tel.: (08 51) 62 40 53

Ankunftstag:
date of arrival – date de l'arrivée

Eingangsstempel

Name (bei Frauen auch Geburtsname) name (maiden name) – nom (née)		Vorname Christian name – prénom	Beruf profession

Geburtsdatum date of birth – date de naissance	Geburtsort place of birth – lieu de naissance	Landkreis	bei ausländischem Geburtsort Staat state – pays	Staatsangehörig nationality – nation

Wohnort residence – domicile	Straße, Hausnummer Nr., street – No., rue	Landkreis	Land, (bei Wohnort im Bundesgebiet: Bundes state – pays

Begleitende Ehefrau: – if accompanied by wife – si accompagné de l'épouse

Vorname Christian name – prénom	geborene maiden name – née	Geburtsdatum date of birth – date de naissance	Geburtsort place of birth – lieu de naissance	Begleitende Kinder: if accompanied by children si accompagné d'enfants

Ritzenburg , den 19

Unterschrift des Gastes – Signature

There was a list of the other offices on the wall, so here are the main ones and what they do:

1. **Das Gesundheitsamt** (Department of Health). Helmut told me he had been there from school when his whole class had been given a medical, and he had gone there too when he had vaccinations against smallpox and polio and for chest X-rays. So it does all the routine examining and testing and vaccinating for which one has to go to a hospital in Britain. It also runs an advisory service for mothers of small children, but there are no family planning or ante-natal clinics – the family doctor looks after expectant mothers.

2. **Das Arbeitsamt** (Labour Office). When I wanted a part-time job I went there to see if I needed a work permit (I didn't). This office also pays out unemployment benefit, and like our Employment Exchanges it can tell you about jobs which are vacant (and not only manual work). But it does far more than this: it provides careers advice for young people, and helps to rehabilitate and re-train those who have been in prison or who have had a bad accident and are partially disabled. So it plays an active part in seeing that everybody who can do a job has one and that the right jobs are available.

3. **Das Finanzamt** (Finance Office). This deals with taxes of every
kind, both those which go to the town and those which go to the state;
it even collects the church tax, which goes to whichever church you
belong to.

Here is a diagram which shows where the town council gets its money
from and where it goes:

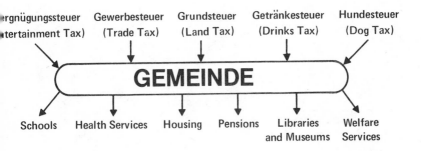

The trade tax *(die Gewerbesteuer)* is paid by all businesses and factories in the town, so the more there are the better off the town is.
Ritzenburg does not have many large firms, so to make up for this the
Land government pays the town some extra money from the taxes
it has taken.

The land tax *(die Grundsteuer)* is paid by every owner of a building
or land and is therefore something like our rates. But it does not cover
refuse collection, drainage, or street cleaning, all of which have to be
paid for separately to the *Stadtwerke* (Public Works Department).

Of course the town gets money in other ways as well–by lending
money and charging interest on it, and from all the services it provides
(water and electricity supplies, rent on the few council properties and
fares from buses and trams). There is no gas supply in Ritzenburg.

4. **Das Sozialamt** (Social Security office) runs the state insurance
scheme for employees. In addition it looks after young and old people
and refugees and visitors from East Germany, as well as doing general
social work.

There are other public offices in the town of course, but it is fairly
obvious from their name what they do–the *Bauamt* issues building
licences and inspects buildings to see that they comply with regula-
tions, while the *Kultur- und Schulamt* is responsible for libraries,
museums, theatres and schools.

After I had digested all this, there was still one question I wanted to ask Helmut. "Where do you have to go to licence a car? Can you do it at a post office?"

"Oh no, you have to go to a special office called the *Kraftfahrzeug-Zulassungsstelle*. I expect you've noticed that most of the cars in Ritzenburg have number plates with RIT followed by another two letters and a number. Those first letters are the registration letters for our *Kreis*. They are usually the first letter or letters of the place name—it's LU for Ludwigshafen for instance:

You can see when the licence needs renewing from the disc on the right. What does the D stand for?

If you move or if you buy a secondhand car registered in another town, you have to take the number plates off and get new ones which are stamped at that office with the long name. You have to be able to show that the car is taxed and insured, and if it's an old one that it's passed its TÜV."

"What's that?"

"It stands for *Technischer Überwachungsverein*—Technical Testing Service. You have to take the car to their local testing station every two years for a very thorough check."

"Oh, I see, much the same idea as our MOT test, except that we have to take our old car every year and we can go to the garage round the corner."

B. Die Polizeiwache

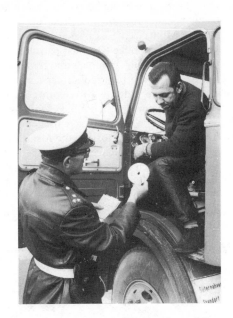

The West German 'Schupo'. This is short for Schutzpolizist, the ordinary policeman as opposed to the plain clothes Kriminalpolizist, who does detective work. On the right he is on traffic duty, checking a lorry driver's papers.

The main police station *(die Polizeiwache)* is in the Bäckerstraße. It is a very ordinary looking building, which can however be recognized by the white shield with a black eagle alongside the door, and the olive green and white police cars parked outside. In addition to the Volkswagen saloons like this one, there are usually Volkswagen vans and

minibuses. Some of these have barred windows for transferring prisoners or taking away people who have been arrested. They are nicknamed 'Grüne Minnas', the equivalent of our 'Black Marias'. Of course the West German police have fast patrol cars *(Streifenwagen)* too, such as BMWs, for chasing criminals and traffic offenders.

The West German policeman in his various uniforms does not seem to be regarded with anything like the same trust which many of us have in our British bobbies. Perhaps this is because so many people only meet him when they have broken the law – he can make you pay an on-the-spot fine for crossing the road when you shouldn't and for parking or speeding offences, while (as we have seen) it is the Ordnungsamt which deals with many routine matters. The German police are aware of this, and had a campaign recently with the old slogan "Der Polizist, dein Freund und Helfer" ('The policeman your friend and helper'). Of course the pistol and rubber truncheon which he often carries do not help.

C. Das Amtsgericht

Next door to the police station is the local court, the *Amtsgericht*. This is the lowest court, a rough equivalent of our Magistrates' Court, since most cases are tried by a judge on his own. But where a sentence has to be passed it often takes the form of a *Schöffengericht*, which means that there are two jurors *(Schöffen)* who help the judge to reach a verdict.

Mostly it is the less serious cases that are tried here – disputes about wills, boundaries, tenancy agreements, etc. and minor offences such as poaching, and claims for damages where the sum involved is not more than DM 1 000. More serious cases are often heard here first, then passed on to a higher court.

6. Transport

A. Introduction

Now as in the Middle Ages Ritzenburg lies on an important route for traffic going from north to south or south to north along the river valley. Today there are many new bridges across the river above and below Ritzenburg, so the east-west traffic does not have to come through the town. The *Autobahn* (motorway), for instance, crosses the river several kilometres to the south of Hallbach.

You can reach Ritzenburg by transport of every kind except for air-craft – by road in a car, bus or lorry (or even in a tram if you are only coming from the outskirts), by rail in a diesel railcar or a train hauled by an electric or diesel engine, and by water in a barge or pleasure steamer.

Looking at the roads first, the main road going north to south runs along the river bank (Uferstraße) and then follows the Hallbacher Landstraße. It is a Bundesstraße (Federal Highway), roughly equivalent to our A roads. It is single carriageway and well surfaced, but not always very wide, particularly where it climbs up into the hills to the north (here there are also many sharp corners). As on all single carriageway roads, you must not drive at more than 100 kilometres per hour ($62\frac{1}{2}$ m.p.h.) outside the town, or more than 50 k.p.h. in the town.

This road on the outskirts of the town still has bumpy Pflastersteine (see p. 7). Also in the picture is the tram's last stop (Endstation)

This road is also called an *Ausfallstraße* because it takes traffic out of the town (as well as bringing it in of course). The other important road out of the town leads to the Autobahn and is called a *Zubringerstraße* (access road). A bypass *(Umgehungsstraße)* has been planned, but it is difficult to find a satisfactory route for it.

The railway also follows the river coming from the north and passes part of the way through the town in a tunnel. It has overhead wires for electric engines, which are used on all important main lines and on most routes in the south of Germany. The main station *(Hauptbahnhof–* abbreviation *Hbf)* is opposite the new bridge across the river.

The river runs from north to south through the town bending eastwards as it does so. It has locks and sluice gates, so that the water flow can be regulated and barges can travel up it to the next big town. There is a lock *(Schleuse)* to the north of the old bridge, and moorings *(Anlegestellen)* for the barges and pleasure boats between the two bridges.

A large barge

B. Ritzenburg Hauptbahnhof

The buildings of the main station are all on one side of the track. There is only one entrance and a subway under the tracks to the different platforms. The main building contains the ticket office *(Fahrkarten- ausgabe)*, left luggage counter *(Gepäckaufbewahrung)* and registered luggage counters–one for sending luggage *(Gepäckannahme)* and one for collecting luggage *(Gepäckausgabe)*. There are also lockers *(Schließ- fächer)* in which you can lock up a case at any time. There is even a restaurant, which is one of the best in the town and stays open very late. Tickets *(Fahrkarten)* are printed on a large electric machine with a pointer which also works out the correct fare. The clerk is behind a heavy glass screen with a perforated metal panel for you to speak

through; you place your money in one half of a swivelling tray and the clerk places the ticket in the other half, on his side of the screen. He turns the tray so you get your ticket (and any change) and he gets your money.

You can have an *einfache Fahrkarte* (single), a *Rückfahrkarte* (return) or a *Zeitkarte* (season). There are special reductions for students as well as young people and people over 65, while a *Bezirkskarte* allows you to go anywhere for a week in the area round Ritzenburg.

If you are travelling overnight you will probably want a couchette *(Liegeplatz)* or a berth in a sleeper *(Schlafwagen)*. These have to be booked in advance, as does a reserved seat of course, for which you buy a *Platzkarte*.

The other day I went with Ursula to visit her cousin Manfred (the one with the prefab). To find out the time of our train we looked at a timetable *(Fahrplan)*, but could not find any trains going there, so we went to the Information Desk *(Auskunft)*. Ursula asked: "Wie kommen wir nach Holzhausen?" (How do we get to Holzhausen?)

The man answered: "Sie müssen in Gießen umsteigen. Sie haben um 14 Uhr einen Zug" (You must change in Gießen. You have a train at 2 p.m.). It was nearly two so we had to run for it.

As the train came in, the announcer said "Vorsicht auf Bahnsteig 1! Der D 508* nach Stuttgart über Gießen hat Einfahrt!" (Take care on

A D-Zug is an express which only stops at the most important stations. The fastest trains are the F-Züge, which cover very long distances (e.g. from Copenhagen to Paris or Hamburg to Zurich), and the Intercity trains which only stop at certain towns and run at high speeds. There are also a few moderately quick trains (Eilzüge), and Personenzüge which are local stopping trains. Diesel railcars (called Schienenbusse) are used on many branch lines and for country services.

Platform 1. The express 508 for Stuttgart via Gießen is coming in).

The platform is low so one has to climb up steps which are at either end of the coach. The train stopped with a screech, and we found ourselves opposite the middle of a coach and had to run to the end to climb in. The coaches are wider than in Britain and quite comfortable, but this is due more to the widespread use of continuously welded rail, I have decided, than to the upholstery, which is fairly firm and covered in serviceable but not very attractive olive green plastic. Only first class compartments are at all plush. We soon found a seat in a non-smoker *(Nichtraucher)* and I sat down rather heavily.

"Ow! This seat is obviously meant for well-padded behinds!"

"You're lucky. Until a few years ago we still had slatted wooden benches on our local trains."

Then the ticket collector *(der Schaffner)* appeared in the doorway. He looked at our tickets, and then explained that this was a D-Zug so we should have paid a supplement *(Zuschlag)* as we were only going a short distance. What's more, since we hadn't paid before getting on, it would be 3 marks instead of 2. We were furious!

C. Buses and trams

Like most German towns, Ritzenburg still has its **tram system** *(die Straßenbahn)*. The trams are modern single-deckers, but each unit is made up of at least two articulated cars and a single tram may consist of more than one unit, looking like a railway train. They can carry more passengers than a bus and are cheaper to run, with good acceleration and brakes (they need these because running on rails they can't get out of the way of other traffic or pedestrians). In some very wide streets (such as the Hallbacher Landstraße or Brückenstraße) they run separately from other traffic in the centre of the roadway with the rails often behind a fence or a hedge.

The trams are electrically driven, and collect their current from overhead wires supported on poles or on brackets fixed to buildings. The driver *(der Fahrer)* sits right at the front. Nowadays he has to check the passengers' tickets as well as drive the tram, as there is no conductor. Most people buy their tickets from a machine provided at the main tram stops, but others have to buy them from the driver. You can imagine they are not very popular in the rush hour!

Most journeys cost the same amount, and the one ticket can be used even if you have to travel on two or more trams to reach your destination. Generally one buys a small booklet of tickets, which is cheaper than buying them singly. Each ticket has a diagram of the route, and the driver punches a hole where you get on. You have to tell him if you want to change *(umsteigen)*.

The driver also operates the folding doors which are at the front for people to get in, and in the middle and at the back for people to get out.

A Gelenkautobus

Buses are run in much the same way – you pay the driver as you get on. Some are in two articulated parts so that they are just like a tram inside (these are called *Gelenkautobusse*). Others tow a separate trailer so that they can carry more passengers; but all are single-deckers. They mostly cater for outlying areas (suburbs and nearby villages). Some are run by the town authorities, but others are run by the Post Office *(Bundespost)* and by the railways. The *Postbusse* are yellow and carry passengers and parcels to villages and farms. So they are the direct successors of the mail coach of olden days, which was also painted yellow (they even have a posthorn as a badge on the front door). The railway buses *(Bahnbusse)* are red and start from the main station. They are partly used to replace train services on branch lines which have been closed, but they cover other routes as well.

The stops *(Haltestellen)* for trams and buses have round signs with a green H in a yellow circle. The numbers of the trams and buses which stop are sometimes displayed below the H. Generally the signs are on poles, but often in the town streets they are fixed to a wall.

There are no orderly queues, people wait around on the pavement and make a rush for the tram or bus when its stops. Sometimes the tram stops in the middle of the road, so that the traffic has to stop to let people get on and off. In the rush hour there is often a free-for-all and the devil take the hindmost! Since the number of standing passengers is not usually restricted, you are all right as long as you can squeeze on before the doors close.

Coaches There are, surprisingly, few regular long-distance coach services within West Germany, although the large *Europabusse* run from the biggest towns to places in other countries.

The Verkehrsamt This is a very useful information office on the Marktplatz. Although primarily a travel bureau, you can also find out here what rooms are available in hotels in Ritzenburg at the counter with the notice ZIMMERNACHWEIS, and what famous sights and other attractions you can see. Tickets can be bought for every kind of transport (trains, buses and trams) and for excursions by coach which start outside the door, as well as for the theatre and concerts. You can also get a plan of the town here, which is very useful if you have just arrived and do not know your way around.

D. Car care

Die Tankstelle

This petrol station is a self-service one, selling petrol at reduced prices. The prices (given in Pfennig per litre) are on the large sign in the background.

Nearly every garage and petrol station has a sign like this. The price at the top is for Diesel, of the other two the bottom price is for *Super* (Premium) and the middle price for *Benzin* (Regular). I objected that it was all Benzin ('petrol'), but Helmut said that the full term for regular *(Normalbenzin)* is hardly ever used now. However a lot of people buy it, because a surprisingly large number of German cars use it.

Out of sight on the left is an automatic car wash *(Waschstraße)*.

There is also a coin-operated petrol station *(Münztankstelle)* on the Weinberger Straße which is open all the time.

Die Garage

Helmut's elder brother Wolfgang has a very good job, so he has bought himself this new Mercedes. However the other day he was overtaken by a BMW, and tried to catch it up. In the process he drove much faster than he should with a new engine, and he has discovered it has used some oil. So now he has a bad conscience and has taken the car to see Herr Bayer at his garage in the Salzgasse for servicing *(Wartung)*. Herr Bayer is very reassuring:

"Don't worry, some engines do use oil when they're running in. But don't do it again–you know there's a limit of 100 kph on the Bundesstraße in any case! The engine seems all right, but take it easy, and I'll have a closer look at the next service if you're still worried."

Meanwhile Fritz, the mechanic, is checking the tyre pressures *(Reifenluftdruck)*. In the workshop *(Werkstatt)* behind him, Helmut's father's car is waiting to be collected after a complete overhaul *(Generalüberholung)*. That's going to be a big bill!

7. Schools

There are several other books which tell you all about the West German education system, here we just want to get some idea of what the schools in Ritzenburg are like.

There are not many nursery schools or kindergartens; and most of those in Ritzenburg are privately run. The largest ones are those run by the main Catholic church *(Marienkirche)* and by the Protestant church *(Johanneskirche)*.

Children at a kindergarten

The first school children go to is the *Grundschule* (primary school), the junior department of the *Volksschule*. The biggest Volksschule in Ritzenburg is the splendid new Georg-Hann-Schule next to the swimming pool *(Schwimmbad)* by the river. Children start going there when they are six; after four years they pass on to a secondary school, of which there are three different sorts:

1. The *Hauptschule*, which is the senior department of the *Volksschule* and takes three-quarters of the children (Helmut and Lisa go to the upper part of the Georg-Hann-Schule);

2. The *Mittelschule*, such as the Rehfußschule in Hallbach, which is something like a Secondary Modern School, for ages 11-16;

3. The *Gymnasium* (grammar school). The biggest one in Ritzenburg is the Bunsengymnasium, which is only for boys and is housed in a large gloomy building in the Altstadt. It was built of pink sandstone in the second half of the 19th century. But although it may look oppressive from the outside, the classrooms are quite light thanks to the high ceilings and tall windows. Also it looks out onto the Stadtpark. Finally we should mention the Katharinenschule, which is a girl's grammar school *(Mädchengymnasium)* on the other side of the river. This is where Ursula goes.

Of these schools only the Georg-Hann-Schule has its own playing field *(Sportplatz)*, since outdoor games are not a very important part of the curriculum. But they all have gymnasiums *(Turnhallen)*, since gymnastics is treated as a special school subject, with periods set aside for it and marks awarded. Games such as netball and handball are played in the gym, while training for athletics and swimming is also organized by the school. They have large playgrounds where the pupils go during break *(die Pause)*, and the new Georg-Hann-Schule has a cafeteria for older pupils where you can get soft drinks etc.

Boys practising handball at the Rehfußschule

There are no private schools in Ritzenburg (apart from the nursery schools), but a few kilometres away there is a *Mädchenpensionat* (girl's boarding school) in a big country house, called Schloß Eisenstein. This is expensive and rather exclusive. However some of the girls go there not purely for snob reasons, but because they have got behind with their lessons. This is sometimes due to moving from another *Land*, where the syllabus is different.

There are also no boarding schools in the town itself, but the Georg-Hann-Schule has a *Landschulheim*–a sort of country hostel–at Langen-bach which is 10 kilometres up the river. Forms go there for a week once a year with their teacher *(Klassenlehrer)*, who is usually worn out at the end of the week. They do not have regular lessons there, but mainly outdoor activities. Senior forms go on long trips with their teacher during term-time, often going abroad to visit famous places or (in the winter) to go skiing. There are also day trips which may involve a long hike in the country or a visit to a famous local building or museum. Forms are sometimes taken to the town theatre *(Stadttheater)* to see plays at special matinee performances for young people *(Jugendvor-stellungen)* and to the concert hall *(Konzertsaal)*, where schools are admitted to the final rehearsal *(Generalprobe)* for a concert.

A Morning at School

One morning Lisa said that if I could get up early enough on Saturday I could go to school with her–her form teacher *(Klassenlehrer)* had said it was all right as long as I sat at the back and kept quiet. I didn't like the idea of going to school on a Saturday, but this is still normal in many German schools.

I met her at 7.30 at the tram stop and squeezed onto the tram with a crowd of schoolboys and girls. Many of the younger ones had the shiny orange satchels and orange caps which make them easy to see on dark mornings.

When we got to the school we went straight to Lisa's classroom—there was no assembly. A shrill bell rang at 8.o and the teacher for the first lesson came in. It was History *(Geschichte)*, and we learnt about Frederick the Great. But first the teacher asked Horst Steingruber, who is the *Klassensprecher* (form spokesman), whether anyone was absent. (Horst is elected by the form and acts as their representative if anything goes wrong). After 55 minutes that bell rang again and we were left on our own for a few minutes before the teacher for the next lesson came. It was the form teacher, who announced that there would be a form outing *(Klassenfahrt)* next week to Marburg to see the castle. Everybody cheered. Then he said there would be a *Klassenarbeit* (class test) the next Tuesday in the form of an English essay. Everybody groaned. I wondered why, so Lisa whispered that they only do a few of these written tests which are marked and count for their overall mark for the year. This decides whether they move up to the next higher form, so these marks are very important. The lesson was English, so the teacher asked me questions about my home and school.

Lisa's Stundenplan (timetable). Rel=Religion, Eng=Englisch, Bio=Biologie, Mu=Musik, Franz=Französisch (French), D=Deutsch (German), Gesch=Geschichte (History), Math=Mathematik, Ch=Chemie, Ph=Physik, Erdk=Erdkunde (Geography), Tu=Turnen (gym), Ku=Kunst (art).

Stundenplan für Lisa Schmidt 10. Klasse

Zeit	Montag	Dienstag	Mittwoch	Donnerstag	Freitag	Samstag
7⁴⁵ – 8³⁰	Rel	D	Gesch	Rel	Mu	Gesch
8³⁵ – 9²⁰	Eng	Gesch	D	Ph	D	Eng
9²⁵ – 10¹⁰	Bio	Math	Bio	D	Math	Erdk
10³⁰ – 11²⁰	Mu	Eng	Erdk	Franz	Tu	Ku
11²⁵ – 12¹⁰	Franz	Ch	Franz	Eng	Tu	Ku
12¹⁵ – 13⁰⁰		Ph			Ch	

At the end of this period there was a short break *(Pause)* and we went out into the yard *(Pausenhof)*, Lisa produced some well filled sandwiches from her briefcase which looked like a business man's. I noticed nearly everybody else was munching away. "Without our *Pausenbrot* we would be starving by the end of the morning."

She was right. Another 3 hours of lessons and I was very hungry indeed. Except for drawing *(Zeichnen)*, we stayed in the same classroom and the teachers came to us. At last it was one o'clock and we all went home. "It seems a very long morning", I said in the tram. "How do the small children manage?" "They don't," was the answer. "At first they only have a couple of lessons then they go home".

I asked Lisa if there was never anything happening at the school in the afternoon and evening.

"Yes, of course. There are a few lessons and all sorts of voluntary activities, including games like netball and handball which you can play in the gym, singing in the school choir and so on. But you don't always *have* to come back in the afternoon, except as a punishment. This is called *Nachsitzen*, and it doesn't happen very often because it is just as much of a punishment for the teacher! Then there are evening classes for adults, organized by the *Volkshochschule*."

So the young people of Ritzenburg have to work hard at their schools, although they have plenty of time to themselves (they have a lot of homework to do though during those 'free' afternoons!). The school as a whole is perhaps less of a community than in Britain. Most activities seem to be restricted to forms, so that pupils from different forms have less opportunity to get to know one another. There is also little swopping between forms; since there is no specialization pupils go on taking all the same subjects until they leave. As a result a pupil may well be with much the same group throughout his or her school career. The only way to get into a different group is by going to another school or doing so badly that he/she is not promoted at the end of the school year. So it is not surprising that reunions of former pupils nearly always take the form of *Klassentreffen*, meetings of people who were together in the same form at school.

When German children leave school, nearly all of them go on to some other form of education. Helmut wants to go into his father's business, so next year he is transferring to the *Handelsschule* (Commercial School), where he will learn book-keeping, typing etc. as well as the usual school subjects. Lisa on the other hand wants to finish at the Hauptschule and then get an apprentice's job *(eine Lehrstelle)* while studying part-time at the *Berufsschule* (Vocational School). This will give her a basic qualification for a job in an office or a shop. Ursula will stay at the Gymnasium until she is 18 to take the *Abitur* exam, which will allow her to go to a University.

8. Recreation and Sport

The largest open space near the centre of the town is the Stadtpark. In one corner there is a children's playground with swings, chutes and a sandpit, with some hard tennis courts and a putting course *(Minigolf)* alongside. The main part of the park consists of sandy paths between stretches of not very well kept grass with shrubs and small trees. Even so, as in all parks, there are plenty of little warning notices such as "Hunde sind an der Leine zu führen" ('Dogs are to be kept on a lead') and "Betreten des Rasens verboten" ('Keep off the grass').

There are also some attractive gardens *(Anlagen)* along the east river bank, and on the other bank to the south of the old town there is a *Liegewiese* – a field running down to the water's edge where you can play games or just lie in the sun. Those who are brave enough and good enough swimmers also swim in the river from here, but the current is strong and the water is not very clean.

The best place to swim is at the splendid new swimming pool *(Schwimmbad)* on the opposite side of the river. This has both an indoor pool *(Hallenbad)* and an outdoor one *(Freibad)*. But Ursula prefers to go to this pool up in the hills behind the castle:

There are two large sports grounds *(Sportplätze)* on the outskirts of the town. One (not shown on the plan) is the football ground of the Ritzenburger Kickers FC, where large crowds gather every Sunday afternoon for the weekly game against one of their rivals in the Regionalliga (regional league). There are five of these leagues for the different parts of the country and they are roughly equivalent in standard to our third and fourth division, but the players are only semi-professional. The club pays them a comparatively small fee, and they have full or part-time jobs as well. Most German clubs are amateur. The only clubs with professional players are those in the national *Bundesliga* (Federal League), and even they do not have paid, full-time managers.

The Ritzenburg club has a junior section, and Helmut is a member. It gives promising young players a chance to develop. This makes up to some extent for the lack of organized sport in the schools, but you have to pay to join and naturally only the best players get a chance of playing in the junior team.

The other ground is a general sports ground for athletics etc. belonging to the Ritzenburger Turnverein (RTV). This means 'Gymnastics Club', but since its formation nearly 100 years ago it has branched out, and now it has sections for most sports.

There is a large variety of other clubs, for all the games we play in Britain (except cricket, of course!), but there is one we must mention for which there is no British equivalent: the *Schützenverein*. This is a shooting club of a very special type, whose traditions go back hundreds of years. Every year they hold a competition *(Schützenfest)* to decide who is the best marksman with a rifle, and he is called the *Schützenkönig*. This is a great occasion for the whole town, with a splendid procession and dancing after the shooting match.

Marksmen with their awards in the procession

Ursula recently got worried about her figure, so Lisa gave her a *Trimm-spirale* and told her to get on with it:

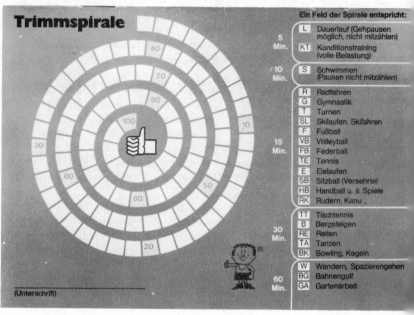

Trimmspirale

Ein Feld der Spirale entspricht:

5 Min.	L Dauerlauf (Gehpausen möglich, nicht mitzählen)
	KT Konditionstraining (volle Belastung)
10 Min.	S Schwimmen (Pausen nicht mitzählen)
15 Min.	R Radfahren
	G Gymnastik
	T Turnen
	SL Skilaufen, Skifahren
	F Fußball
	VB Volleyball
	FB Federball
	TE Tennis
	E Eislaufen
	SB Sitzball (Versehrte)
	HB Handball u. ä. Spiele
	RK Rudern, Kanu
30 Min.	TT Tischtennis
	B Bergsteigen
	RE Reiten
	TA Tanzen
	BK Bowling, Kegeln
60 Min.	W Wandern, Spazierengehen
	BG Bahnengolf
	GA Gartenarbeit

(Unterschrift)

"What do I have to do?" asked Ursula.

"You have to fill in the 100 squares, one at a time, after you have done one of the sporting activities listed for the length of time shown. You put the letters in the squares to show what you have done—S for 10 minutes' swimming, TE for 15 minutes' tennis, TA for 30 minutes' dancing . . ."

"Dancing? That's a good idea! I'll just have to go to the disco every night for the next three months or so."

"I don't think that's quite the idea. And anyway who's going to dance with you every night for three months? And it'll come rather expensive, won't it?"

"Oh well, I'll go swimming and do some extra gym, and I'll get out my bicycle again—at least that doesn't cost anything. And where do I send the spiral when it's filled in?"

"To the Deutscher Sportbund—they're running this campaign called *Trimm Dich durch Sport* ('Keep fit through sport'). When they get it they send you a badge with a spiral on it."

"Up in the woods behind the castle they've recently laid out a special course called a *Waldsportpfad*, which involves a whole series of exercises. You just run from one to the next until you've finished—or you're finished! Perhaps you could try that once a week as well?" suggested Helmut.

9. Entertainment and Culture

A. Theatre and concerts

One of the most surprising things about a small German town like Ritzenburg is the number and high standard of theatre performances and concerts. It is unlikely that a British town of this size would have a theatre at all, let alone an orchestra.

The town theatre *(Stadttheater* or *Städtische Bühne)* puts on everything from straight plays and operas to musicals and operettas. It is a repertory theatre with a small permanent company, but unlike British repertory theatres it does not put on the same show for a week or a fortnight and then change to something else. At any given time, they have as many as six different plays and other shows which they can put on, so occasionally you can see six different programmes in one week! There are performances every evening including Sunday, but not on Mondays (this is their 'rest day', although much hard work goes on with rehearsals). Some performances are given for particular clubs, such as the *Jugendring* for young people, or you can buy a *Platzmietekarte*, a sort of season ticket which allows you to buy tickets at a special low rate for a whole series of performances. What's more, you can pay for it in instalments! Naturally a theatre in a town of this size could not make enough money, so like all West German theatres the one in

Ritzenburg receives a subsidy (*i.e.* financial help) from the state and town authorities. It is run by an *Intendant,* who is responsible for the business side as well as engaging actors and producers, deciding what plays to do and even producing some of them himself.

The building itself is an old one, going back to the early nineteenth century. It is also quite small, with only simple stage equipment. But this means that it has a pleasantly friendly atmosphere.

When I went to the box office *(die Kasse),* I found I had the following choice:

Parkett 1.–6. Reihe	DM 10.00	(Stalls Rows 1–6)	
7.–14. Reihe	DM 7.00	Rows 7–14)	
1. Rang Mitte 1.–3. Reihe	DM 10.00	(Dress Circle Centre	
		Rows 1–3)	
4.–6. Reihe	DM 6.00	Rows 4–6)	
Seite	DM 5.00	Side)	
2. Rang 1.–3. Reihe	DM 5.00	(Upper Circle Rows 1–3)	
4.–6. Reihe	DM 3.00	Rows 4–6)	
Stehplatz	DM 1.50	(Standing room)	

I wanted to give Ursula a treat, so I bought two tickets in the Erster Rang for *Die Zauberflöte* (The Magic Flute), but I found they were even more than I expected – the opera prices are higher.

On entering the theatre, the first thing I noticed was that almost everyone was dressed up in his or her Sunday best. Theatregoing is still an occasion in Germany. I found we were also expected to hand over our coats to the cloakroom attendant, but there was no fee; "You only tip them if you want to", explained Ursula. During the interval I was also surprised to see people walking up and down in orderly rows in the wide corridors, forming a long procession. This is a survival from the days when ladies promenaded with their partners so that people watching could admire them in their finery.

I noticed the same thing when I went to a concert. The Germans are a very musical people, and the concerts in the Hermelinsaal, the town's concert hall, are well attended. Except, that is, when there is too much modern music in the programme; as in other countries, audiences in a small town tend to be conservative. Some concerts are given by the Municipal Orchestra *(Städtisches Orchester)* and others by visiting orchestras and soloists. The most important are the subscription concerts; if you buy tickets for a whole series, they come much cheaper.

In the summer, the hard working Municipal Orchestra (which is also the theatre orchestra) gives outdoor concerts *(Serenadenkonzerte)* in the gardens of the castle, which makes a wonderful setting. There are also splendid choral concerts and organ recitals in the town's churches, especially at Christmas and Easter.

What about jazz and pop groups, you may ask. Well, there are occasional concerts by visiting celebrities, and there is one night club where good jazz can be heard, but most music-making of this kind is provided by the young people themselves. The big groups naturally keep to the largest cities.

However, a discotheque has just opened in one of the small streets near the station, and it is very popular. It is called 'Der Oldtimer' (by which the Germans mean an old car, not an old person!) I went there one evening with Lisa and Helmut and Ursula. It was very enjoyable, but I was puzzled when I was asked for my *Ausweis* (identity card) as we were going in. I handed over my passport, which I fortunately had with me. Lisa explained that all those under 18 have to leave at 10, and if they have not left by then, their names are called out, which makes them feel very small.

There is probably rather more night life in Ritzenburg than in a similar British town. There are one or two bars which stay open until the early hours of the morning, where you can dance on a tiny, dimly lit dance floor, while even the ordinary pubs and restaurants *(Gasthäuser)* stay open until the *Polizeistunde* (closing time) of 1 a.m.

Das Kino

The main cinema in Ritzenburg is the Burgtheater, which is near the castle. Helmut said there was a good Western on there, so we all went along on Saturday afternoon. There was a short queue, and we had the usual argument about which seats to go for.

These were the prices:

1. Parkett	DM 4.00	1. Sperrsitz	DM 5.00
2. Parkett	DM 4.50	2. Sperrsitz	DM 5.50
	Balkon	DM 6.00	

I was puzzled by the names, so Ursula explained: *"Parkett* means front stalls and *Sperrsitz* rear stalls; *Balkon* you can guess! The 1. stands for *erstes* or *erster* (first) and 2. for *zweites* or *zweiter* (second)."

We got 2. Parkett, but had to wait a few minutes until the first programme ended; the tickets are only for one showing, so you cannot go in during one programme and leave in the middle of the next one.

It seemed odd watching cowboys talking in German, but I soon got used to it. Helmut told me that nearly all foreign films are dubbed in Germany. I was also surprised to find nobody smoking – it's strictly forbidden in German cinemas.

Die Stadtbibliothek

The municipal library is housed in a fine new building in the Hallbacher Landstraße, close to the station. You can borrow books for two weeks at 10 Pfennig a time, but students who need them for their work don't have to pay. However there is a high charge for books kept longer than 2 weeks without renewal (2 marks), which applies to everybody. I told the librarian Herr Stolz that we don't have to pay for library books in this country. "In some bigger towns there are free libraries," he said, "but a small town like Ritzenburg can't afford to lend books for nothing."

Next to the main library is a children's library *(Jugendbibliothek)*.

Das Museum

Ursula said if I was interested in local crafts such as pottery and weaving I should go to the town museum, which is what is called a *Heimatmuseum*. This means that it shows only things connected with the town and the surrounding district. We would probably call it a local history museum.

It is in an old house in the Johannesstraße. I particularly liked the rooms which are furnished in the styles of different periods; there is one made to look like an old farmhouse kitchen with the typical brightly painted *Bauernmöbel*–large blue cupboards and chests with red flowers on them. The historical section also had some archaeological finds– Roman coins and bits of pottery, as well as later coins–plus a selection of costumes, jewellery, glass and silver. In another room there is a collection of old masks which are taken out every year in February for the Carnival procession. Then there are pictures of famous people who lived in Ritzenburg, with paintings by local artists and books by local writers. For a complete change you can go through to the natural history section which has all the animals you can expect to see in the fields and forests round Ritzenburg (stuffed, of course), and to the geology room where you can see specimens of different sorts of rock and diagrams of the local hills.

10. Eating, Drinking and Sleeping

A. Das Café

The smarter German cafés have changed little over the years. If you go into Café-Konditorei Döring in the Hauptstraße at about 3.30 in the afternoon, you will see much the same scene as before the war. This is the time of the ceremonial *Nachmittagskaffee* (afternoon coffee). Many of the customers are middle-aged ladies wearing plain round hats and rather shapeless (but spotlessly clean) clothes. They tend to be rather plump, which is not surprising in view of their fondness for cream cakes. What is more, they eat these with a large portion of whipped cream. Lisa's mother, Frau Schmidt, comes here every other day to meet her friends. Then in the summer she goes on a special slimming course . . .

The whole place is very clean, and furnished in neutral colours (white, beige and cream). There is a long refrigerated counter down one side, in which the wonderful display of cakes can be seen. But first of all you go to your table and order your coffee (or tea if you want to be different). The coffee *(Kaffee)* usually comes in a pot *(Kanne)* on a tray with a cup and saucer and a tiny jug of cream. This cream *(Kaffeesahne)* is a special kind of condensed milk, and the coffee is very strong. In contrast the tea is weak, and often served in a glass with a slice of lemon *(Tee mit Zitrone* – what we call Russian tea). Then you go to the counter and choose your cakes. You don't have to have a piece of cream cake, since there are also *Obsttorten* (fruit flans made with fresh fruit), cheesecake *(Käsekuchen)* and quite plain small cakes (see p. 24 for more details).

A tempting display of cakes and ices

But one has to admit that the cream cakes are superb! In the summer one can also have ices, and sit outside:

Incidentally, the Konditorei in the title means that they make their own cakes and that you can buy them to take home.

The smaller, less smart cafés are more like those in Britain (but do not provide cooked meals, of course). You will also see more young people in them.

Die Eisdiele

Yesterday I met Ursula at the ice cream parlour *(Eisdiele)* in the Lindenhammer Straße, one of the streets leading from the Market Place. It was full of young people. "It's popular because you can buy delicious Italian-type water ices here in all sorts of flavours, and they are quite cheap," said Ursula. "Also you can buy an ice and sit for hours just talking with your friends."

"What make are the ices?"

"Their own make of course, they make them here on the premises."

I could not decide which to have, so I had a mixture of banana, nut and coffee flavours. My ice came in a metal cup, but Ursula's came in a glass. It was an *Eisbecher* (sundae) consisting of ice cream, fruit, nuts etc. and topped with whipped cream, as in the picture opposite.

Die Imbißstube

This little snack bar opposite the station is much the same as a British one in appearance, but it sells different things: beer, for instance, and *Bratwurst* (a large fried sausage).

B. Das Gasthaus

The German *Gasthaus* is a cross between a pub and a restaurant. (If it is called a *Gaststätte*, it is probably fairly smart and concentrates more on food). You sit at a table as in a restaurant, and a waiter or waitress brings your order. But particularly in the evening a lot of people go there only to drink, because like the café and the English pub it is an important meeting place, especially for men. Or if you just want to be quiet you can sit and read the papers. Both local and national papers are usually provided, often clamped in wooden holders and hanging on coathooks.

There are many delightful Gasthäuser in the old town and we wanted to go to one, but it was shut (there was a notice in the window saying *Donnerstag Ruhetag*, 'shut on Thursdays'). Zum roten Adler (literally 'At the sign of the Red Eagle') in the Burgstraße, where we went in the end, is more typical of what you find all over Germany.

We go in through a swing door with green glass in its top half. We then find ourselves in a large room. Some of the tables are uncovered, but very clean. The short bar *(die Theke)* has a polished copper top and a machine with taps for pouring beer. There is no one standing at it except for a waiter *(Kellner)* waiting for 3 glasses of beer to be filled.

The square windows have large panes of yellow glass similar to the green glass in the door and you cannot see through them although they let in the light. The woodwork is all varnished, with benches along the roughcast walls. The lights are imitations of oil lamps made of brass and yellowish glass hanging from wooden beams. Thus the interior is very traditional in style and not so very different from the old Gasthäuser, except that the wood is light and new instead of dark and old. One of the tables near the bar has a flag on it with 'Stammtisch' written on it. "That's for certain select, regular customers and friends of the landlord *(der Wirt)*," Herr Krüger told me.

We sit down at a table nearby and Herr Krüger orders our beer from the waiter by calling "Herr Ober". "It's short for 'Herr Oberkellner'," Herr Krüger explains. "This waiter may not be the head waiter, but it's always best to be flattering."

What kind of beer do you want?
Ein Helles–a light draught beer, generally with more taste and
   less gassy than the 'Lager' sold in Britain.
Ein Dunkles–a dark sweet beer with low alcohol content (also
   called *Malzbier*).
Pilsner–or **Export**–a strong bottled beer.
Weißbier–a light, rather gassy beer made with wheat malt (only
   obtainable in certain places).

The children at the next table are drinking *Apfelsaft* (apple juice) and Coca Cola. I am surprised to see such young children, but Frau Krüger laughs. "There is no law to stop them coming into Gasthäuser. It's only you English who make life difficult for parents."

Our beer comes, and I notice that the glass is not full to the top. But again there is nothing wrong; a space has to be left for the froth, since German beer is quite fizzy. "It's very cold", I object "which is refreshing in summer, but doesn't it get too much of a good thing in the winter?"

"Yes, some people ask for a *Bierwärmer*. That's a tube filled with hot water, which makes the beer a little less icy," replies Ursula.

The people at the next table have a second round of beer, and the waiter makes two marks on their beer mats. Herr Krüger smiles, since I look puzzled. "It's one mark for each drink. When they've finished, the waiter will examine the beer mat to see how much they owe. It's an old custom, which is going out now."

A selection of beer mats

Now it is time to look at the menu *(die Speisekarte)* which I had already seen displayed in a glass case on the wall outside. This one is called *die Tageskarte*, because it is different every day. It shows first the set meals at all-in prices for soup, main dish and dessert *(Gedecke* or *Menüs)* :

Inh. Heinz Bauer

Gaststätte

Zum roten Adler

Ritzenburg   Burgstr. 26

T a g e s k a r t e

29. November 1974

M E N Ü S :

Kraftbrühe mit Einlage Bratwurst "ungarisch" m. Salat u. Salzkartoffeln, Dessert DM 6.50	Kraftbrühe mit Einlage Kalbsfrikassée auf Butter - reis, Spargel u. Champignons, Dessert DM 9.50
Kraftbrühe mit Einlage Geflügelleber im Purée- rand und Salat, Dessert DM 7.50	Kraftbrühe mit Einlage Forelle "blau" m. zerl. Butter, Salat u. Salz- kartoffeln, Dessert DM 10.00
Kraftbrühe mit Einlage Eisbein auf Weinkraut und Kartoffelpurée, Dessert DM 8.00	Kraftbrühe mit Einlage Schweineschnitzel m. Blu- menkohl u. Pommes frites Dessert DM 10.00
Kraftbrühe mit Einlage Schweinebraten m. Apfel- rotkraut u. Salzkartoffeln, Dessert DM 8.50	Kraftbrühe mit Einlage Kalbskotelett m. Stangen- spargel, Butterkartoffeln, Dessert DM 10.50

Kinderteller:

Kalbsfrikassée im Reisrand mit Champignons und Spargel   DM 6.00

There follow the separate dishes which are ready cooked *(Tagesgerichte* or *fertige Speisen)*. These include today's special, which is marked "Heute besonders zu empfehlen". Then on another page is the printed list of dishes which are always available *(die feste Speisekarte)*, and finally a list of drinks *(Getränke)*. Most of these are familiar, but I have to ask what *Offene Weine* are. "Those are just the wines you can have by the glass," replies Herr Krüger.

All the dishes on the menu are German, although I notice some Italian and French names such as *Risotto* and *Ragout* and *Frikassee*, but even these seem to be used for German recipes. So I wonder whether there are any restaurants specializing in non-German food, like the Indian and Chinese and Italian restaurants at home.

"Oh no Roy, not in Ritzenburg," says Ursula. "We don't even have a French one. You have to go to a bigger town for exotic food."

After the usual difficulty in making up my mind, I decide to have *Schweinebraten* (roast pork), because I know what that is. The others order *Eisbein*. "What on earth is 'ice leg'?" I ask. "It sounds horrible."

"You don't know what's good. It's a knuckle of pork specially pickled and in its own jelly."

The soup soon comes, not in the plates, but in metal cups, whose contents are emptied into the soup plates at the table. The *Einlage* (extra ingredient) turns out to be noodles. The main dish is also brought to the table in separate dishes, so that we can put as much or as little on our plates as we want.

As usual, the vegetables are not just boiled but specially prepared. My red cabbage, for instance, has been cooked very slowly with vinegar, onion and apple. The others have decided to have a salad, so they ask for a *gemischter Salat* (*Salat* by itself, Herr Krüger explains, means just lettuce). Their salad comes in a separate glass dish and is already covered in a dressing. I have boiled potatoes *(Salzkartoffeln)* and the others mashed *(Kartoffelpuree)*; one can also have chips *(Pommes frites)* or fried potatoes *(Bratkartoffeln)*.

The sweet *(Nachtisch)* at the end of the meal is the one disappointment. There is no choice and it turns out to be what the Germans call *Pudding*, a kind of tasteless blancmange. "We're not very good at sweets," Ursula admits. "It's usually either this or stewed fruit *(Kompott)*".

When we have all finished, Herr Krüger calls "Herr Ober, bitte zahlen." The bill is quite a big one, made even bigger by 10% service *(Bedienung)* and VAT *(Mehrwertsteuer)*.

Die Weinstube

A few days later it was Lisa's birthday, so we went to the *Schnitzelbank* in the Johannesstraße to celebrate. This is a simple little wine parlour with quite plain decor and furniture, but the wine is very good. Most people drink it by the Viertel (a large $\frac{1}{4}$ litre glass) but we decided to buy a bottle between the four of us.

The label said "1971er Deidesheimer Herrgottsacker Spätlese–naturrein–Originalabfüllung" and then the name of the vintner. "It means the grapes from which the wine is made were picked in 1971 in the Herrgottsacker vineyard in Deidesheim, a village on the Weinstraße to the west of the Rhine, fairly late in the year–October or early November *(Spätlese)*. The "naturrein" shows it contains no extra additives (sugar for instance) and *Originalabfüllung* means it was bottled by the vineyard owner", explained Helmut, the wine expert. "You can find out a lot from a wine label!"

"I've also seen Riesling or Sylvaner on a label. What are they?"

"Those are different kinds of grape."

"Is there any wine made in and around Ritzenburg?"

*The Schnitzelbank is on the right – you can see the sign.
In the background is the Heimatmuseum.*

"No, but you don't have to go far. A famous area for wine is near Würzburg on the Main, and not all that far to the west is the part of the Rhine where most German wine comes from."

The bottle came with four tall glasses with thin stems, called *Römer* because they are something like the goblets the Romans drank from. We all raised our glasses to drink Lisa's health, saying "Herzliche Glück-wünsche zum Geburtstag" ('Happy Birthday') instead of the more usual "Prost" or "Zum Wohl".

C. Sleeping
Das Hotel Die Pension

The small Hotel Kronenmüller in the Breslauer Straße is much the same as a British private hotel, but it is a *Hotel garni*, which means it does not serve any meals apart from breakfast. This is a feature it shares with the guesthouses in the town, such as the Pension Bauer in the Goethestraße near the station. This is a modest but reasonably comfortable place to stay and costs much less than a hotel.

There is only one large hotel with its own restaurant, the Parkhotel Schmidt. It stands in its own grounds in the Weinberger Straße and is of course very expensive.

Der Gasthof

The Gasthof zum Löwen in a street leading off the Marktplatz is exactly the same as a Gasthaus downstairs. You come through the door into a large restaurant; since it is very old, the ceiling is low and the wood is all blackened with age. But upstairs it has rooms for overnight visitors, so that it is a cross between a Gasthaus and a hotel.

Die Jugendherberge

The youth hostel is housed in a large old villa above the river on the Feldbergweg. It is of course the cheapest place to stay, but very clean and friendly. Everyone will address you as 'du', including the *Herbergsvater*, who runs it and will greet you on arrival.

11. Three Public Services

A. Die Müllabfuhr

Early one morning I was woken up by a lot of banging followed by a hissing noise, with the rumble of an engine in the background. Can you guess what it was? This is what I saw:

Refuse collection in Germany is highly organized. The dustbins (*Mülleimer*) are a standard pattern and size, and fit on a platform at the back of the dustcart. This lifts them up and tips them so that the rubbish falls into the dustcart. The hissing noise comes from the compressed air mechanism which lifts the dustbins and then brings them down again when they are empty. They also have hinged lids which can't fall off and get lost.

Another dustcart came later to pick up the refuse from the shop next door, which has some larger containers on wheels, which the dustmen trundled out and pushed onto another kind of platform. Then the same thing happened – the heavy container swung up into the air and was shaken until it was empty, then down it came again. All very simple, and no mess.

Even so, my landlady Frau Hennewig complains about the dustmen, but I think this is mainly because one has to pay a separate fee for their services, and then you still have to put your dustbin out for them!

B. Die Feuerwehr

Just round the corner from where I am staying is a yard with what looks like a large garage. I asked Ursula what it was and she said it was the *Spritzenhaus,* and I was puzzled since I knew *Spritze* means injection, but that building didn't look like a hospital.

So I asked what was kept in those garages.

"The fire engines of course," was the answer.

"It belongs to our voluntary fire brigade–the Freiwillige Feuerwehr Ritzenburg. It's made up of voluntary part-time firemen. Why don't you ask Rolf? His father's in it."

I did ask Rolf. It turns out that these voluntary firemen have certain days when they are liable for duty; but even on these days they just work at their jobs in the normal way until the siren sounds, then they drop everything and dash to the fire station or the fire. You would think that a house could burn down before they arrived, but the system seems to work all right, and is the normal one in all small towns and villages. Particularly in a village, it is quite an honour to be a member. And every summer they have a tremendous party–the *Feuerwehrfest:*

C. Das Krankenhaus

There are two hospitals in Ritzenburg, the large new Allgemeines Krankenhaus on the Uferstraße and the older Catholic Josefsspital on the Waldheimer Weg near the castle.

Triplets in incubators watched by a nursing nun

When I went past the Josefsspital I noticed there were a lot of nuns around. Lisa told me that all the nursing staff there are nuns. "But you don't have to be a Catholic to be taken in as a patient, although probably most of the people who go there are."

"And what about the Allgemeines Krankenhaus? Is that run by Protestants then?"

"Oh no, that was built by the town with assistance from the rest of the *Kreis*. There are hospitals run by the Protestant Church in other places though. The A.K. has doctors and nurses from all over the place. You must meet my Greek friend Mikis."

Mikis told me that a lot of his friends from Greece had come to work in West German hospitals. "The money is good and the standards are high. But we have to work very hard."

"Is Greece the only country outside Germany that doctors come from?"

"Oh no, I know Persians, Turks, Egyptians and Afghans, and there must be other nationalities. They come here to study and stay on to work. And the Krankenschwestern–the nurses–come from all over the place too–from Korea and Indonesia for instance, and the Mediterranean countries."

"I think there are a lot of people from these countries in factories here too."

"Yes, they're called *Gastarbeiter*. They cannot get jobs in their own countries, or only poorly paid ones, so they come here and often take the humdrum jobs in factories and hospitals for which it is difficult to find people."

"And how about hospital treatment here–does one have to pay for it?"

"Not usually. Everybody pays contributions and belongs to a health insurance scheme *(Krankenkasse)*, either to the Allgemeine Orts- krankenkasse (AOK), the local organization which runs the state health insurance scheme, or to one of the special ones for different kinds of job, or to a private scheme. When you need treatment you go to the Krankenkasse and get a certificate *(der Krankenschein)*. This allows you to go to the doctor or specialist you want to see without paying. But if you go to hospital the AOK only pays for third class treatment. If you want to have a room to yourself (that's *erste Klasse*–first class) or to share a room with only one or two others *(zweite Klasse*, second class), obviously you have to pay the extra amount. Unless, that is, you belong to a private insurance scheme as well. Many people do, because they want to be more comfortable if they have to go to hospital, and some firms even pay the additional contributions for all their employees automatically. But things are changing–some new hospitals only have one class of accommodation."

The Allgemeines Krankenhaus
with a Mercedes ambulance outside

12. Das Postamt

The West German postal authority is *die Bundespost*. It is responsible for much the same services as the British Post Office, but it also runs some country buses (see p. 40). The largest post office *(Postamt)* in Ritzenburg is in the Burgstraße.

Outside there are a letter box *(Briefkasten* or *Briefeinwurf)*, stamp machines *(Briefmarkenautomaten)* and phone boxes *(Telefonzellen)*. All these are painted yellow, like the German mail vans and post buses. On the letter box it says: *Nächste Leerung* (next collection) and then the time. The stamp machines tell you what coins to put in *(e.g.* "2 × 10 Pf") alongside the slot, and have a handle to wind. A bell rings as the stamp comes out.

From some phone boxes you can only make local calls *(Ortsgespräche)* and from some others long-distance calls *(Ferngespräche)* (these will always be STD and not through the operator). But from most phone boxes you can make any kind of call.

Inside the post office there is a long counter divided into sections called *Schalter* with glass partitions in between. In each section an employee sits sideways on to the counter with money, stamps, forms, etc. in front of him or her *(not* on the counter). Above each section there is a notice which says what you can get from that particular employee.

I want to post three letters to England, plus a small parcel and a large one, so first I go to a counter with a notice saying "Postwertzeichen in kleinen Mengen" (stamps in small quantities). I ask for three 70 Pfennig stamps (Drei Marken zu 70 Pfennig), and put the small parcel *(das Päckchen)* on the scales *(die Waage)* which are on the counter. Then I say "Einschreiben bitte" ('Registered please'). The big parcel *(das Paket)* I have to take to the parcels counter, where I find you cannot register parcels.

West German postmen *(Briefträger)* wear a blue uniform and have a leather satchel in which they carry the letters for delivery. Some still ride bicycles which are painted yellow (of course!). However many of them now drive round in vans. They stop at a convenient point and take out a folding trolley *(Roller)*, with which they go from door to door delivering the letters. Special postmen called *Geldbriefträger* are responsible for delivering money which has been paid in at a post office for someone in another town. To do this you buy a *Postanweisung* for the amount you want to send, or fill in a *Zahlkarte* if you have a *Postscheckkonto*, which is something like a postal Giro account.

*A combined letter box
and stamp machine*

A phone box

Inside the main post office

13. Die Bank

The local branch of the Deutsche Bank is in a large important-looking building near the post office. As in the post office, the counter is divided into Schalter. You will probably only go in to change a traveller's cheque *(Reisescheck)*. You show it to one clerk who asks you to sign it, and when the amount in marks has been worked out he gives you a slip and says "Zur Kasse, bitte". You then go with the slip to the cashier who pays out the money.

The process is much the same for people like Wolfgang who have an account *(das Konto)* at the bank and want to take money out. He fills in a withdrawal slip and hands it over to a clerk, who checks it and passes it on to the cashier, who pays out the money.

Every time money is taken out of Wolfgang's account or paid into it, the bank sends him a statement to show how much money he has got. This service must cost the banks a lot, but it is very valuable to know all the time just how much money you have.

You may see gold coins displayed in the bank. These are not used as normal currency, but are bought as an investment. Gold becomes more and more valuable from year to year. (Some people also do this in Britain. What are our gold coins called?) There are also notices showing today's share prices and the exchange rates of the most important currencies.

A scene in a small bank

Sparen wie im Schlaf.

Per Dauerauftrag.

Sparen lassen. Per
Dauerauftrag. Bei der
Sparkasse. Denn wer
automatisch spart,
spart automatisch mehr.

wenn's um Geld geht
Sparkasse

Die Sparkasse

The Germans are great savers. Most towns have several savings banks
(Sparkassen). In Ritzenburg the largest one is the Landessparkasse in
the Marktstraße. You can of course borrow money from it as well as
pay it in, but only if you have a savings account there. It runs a special
savings scheme with bonuses for regular savers. This is called
Prämiensparen.

There is also a *Bausparkasse* (a kind of building society) in the
Brückenstraße which helps you save for a house, but unlike our building societies it does not lend you money to buy any house you want. You
may have to have one of those specially designed for the society. Also,
as with the Sparkasse, you can often only borrow money if you have
had a savings account for some time.

14. Die Zeitung

Every town of any size in Germany has its own newspaper, which contains not only local news but also reports on world events. Ritzenburg is no exception. The *Ritzenburger Rundschau* appears daily and is bought by most families in the town and in the surrounding area. This is all the more surprising since we do not have to buy it in order to read it; a copy is obligingly displayed in the windows of the paper's office on the corner of the Hauptstraße and the Marktplatz, and it can also be read in most cafés and Gasthäuser.

The front page and the two following pages cover the latest world events. Naturally a small local paper such as this does not have reporters all over the world, so these reports are written up from material provided by the central news agencies. The fourth and fifth pages are devoted to sport, again with world coverage, but concentrating on German events and especially local fixtures. The rest of the paper contains local news, general articles including a 'leader' *(Leitartikel)*, and of course advertisements and announcements of what's on at the theatre, the cinema and so on.

At the weekend, there is a special extra section called the *Feuilleton*, which is more like a magazine, and contains all kinds of general articles.

I asked Heinz Lindner, one of the reporters, why the *Rundschau* is so popular with people in the town.

"I think it's partly habit – they've always bought it and so they go on buying it – and partly loyalty: they feel a duty to support it, because after all it provides a valuable service. We tell them everything they want to know for only 50 Pfennig a day!"

Here are some small ads:

15. Zwei Kirchen

There are several fine churches in Ritzenburg, about half of them Catholic *(katholisch)* and half Protestant *(evangelisch)*. Nearly all German Protestants are either Lutherans or belong to the Reformed Church. Here in Central Germany there are slightly more Protestants than Catholics, whereas in the south and in the Rhineland there are far more Catholics and in the north far more Protestants.

A. Die Johanneskirche

This is one of the oldest churches in the town, a tall Gothic church dating from the 14th and 15th centuries. There is no churchyard round it. Some old gravestones and many beautifully carved memorials are placed round the outside of the walls, and these must once have stood in a churchyard.

People are only buried in the large cemetery *(Friedhof)* on the outskirts of the town nowadays. Very few German churches, either in country or town, have their own graveyards.

A roadside sign giving times of church services

The Johanneskirche

Inside, the church is quite plain since this is a Protestant church (*Evangelische Kirche*). It has tall pillars and high windows climbing up to the roof, both the pillars and the walls being of pink sandstone. There are no paintings, but a number of memorials.

A service was just starting when I went in, so I stayed. The pastor (*der Pastor*), who wore a plain black cassock with just two white strips hanging down from the neck, took the whole service by himself. The choir was out of sight up in the organ gallery. The strangest thing, I found, was that the congregation sat down while singing the hymns and stood up for the prayers. Otherwise the service is similar to that of our Presbyterian Church and Church of Scotland, which is not surprising because they have similar ideas to the German Lutheran and Reformed Churches.

B. Die Marienkirche

This is the chief Roman Catholic church in the town. It was built originally even earlier than the Johanneskirche, having been part of the monastery. But in the early 18th century it was almost completely rebuilt inside in the Baroque style. So while it is plain outside, the interior is a blaze of light and colour, with almost every surface covered in paintings or decorated. In addition to the magnificent main altar, which has a beautiful oil painting in an elaborate structure with pillars and statues of saints, there are several altars along each side of the church, each one for a different saint.

Ursula took me to mass there last Sunday. I noticed that there were several priests taking part in the service, who wore magnificent robes. All the altars had candles burning on them, and in front of a picture of the Virgin Mary were rows of candles *(Votivkerzen)* put there by people who have been praying for something. (There was a supply of candles nearby and a box to put the money in).

During the service two collections were taken, the sidesmen coming round with bags on the end of long poles. Many people wandered in after the mass had started and some left before it had ended. As we went out I looked at the notice board and saw a list of the films which were being shown at the local cinema that month. Alongside were short opinions and a rating of the value of the film. I asked Ursula if this was normal.

"Oh yes, the church is always trying to stop people going to really bad films and to point out what it thinks is good or bad about others. It wants to protect Catholics from what it thinks could be a harmful influence. But plenty of them still go to see sex films, whatever the church may say."

"What exactly is that place called the Kolpinghaus behind the church? There seem to be a lot of young people there."

"It's a hostel run by the church mainly for young Catholics who are living away from home. They can have a room and eat there for very little. The idea was started by a bishop called Kolping for apprentices who were learning a job away from home. Now a lot of students live there too."

"I see, something like a YMCA."

"Not quite, since it's mainly for Catholics. Our equivalent of the YMCA is the CVJM – *Christliche Vereinigung Junger Männer.*"

Questions and Project Work

1. History

A. Find out about the history of your town or village. How is it different from that of Ritzenburg?

B. Choose a real West German town, and by looking it up in encyclopedias and writing for brochures etc. find out about its history. Then write a short account of how it developed.

C. Who was St. Boniface? Find out where he came from and when he lived.

D. Why did the Romans build the *limes?* Who were the enemies they wanted to hold back?

E. Find a picture of a real castle and describe it. Why were castles often built on hills? What did they often have round them?

F. Find out about the Thirty Years' War in a history book. Who was fighting whom?

G. Find some pictures of Baroque buildings and describe them. Why do you think they were built in such a magnificent style?

H. When did Ritzenburg grow very fast? And why?

I. Why do the barges need a lock to go up the river? What sort of cargo do they carry?

2. Streets

A. What are the differences between the old streets and the newer streets in Ritzenburg?

B. Describe the streets in an old town which you know.

C. Does other traffic have to give way to a tram? Why, do you think? And on which side do cars usually overtake a tram?

D. What do you have to watch out for on a pedestrian crossing? Can you cross at any time? When?

E. List the differences between British and German traffic lights.

F. Where can you park in Ritzenburg but not in a British town? Is this a good idea, do you think?

3. Houses and flats

A. Have you ever seen a half-timbered house in England? (if not, find a picture of one). What differences do you notice between it and the German houses in the picture? Why are they called *half*-timbered, do you think?

B. Why doesn't one want too much snow on the roof? And why doesn't one want all the snow to slide off at once?

C. Can you walk straight into a German apartment building or block of flats? Why not? How do you get in?

D. What are the disadvantages of the Krüger's flat?

E. What sort of people live in the *Villen?* Are they afraid of burglars, do you think? Why?

F. List the different sorts of windows mentioned. Do you see any of these in Britain? If so, where? What advantages or disadvantages do they have compared with the windows in your home?

G. What are the differences between a Schukostecker and a British earthed plug?

H. Why do Germans insist on having a cellar? What is it useful for?

I. Describe a visit to some friends in a modern German house.

4. Shops

A. You have a shopping list with the following items; which specialist shops do you have to go to? (give the German names):

$\frac{1}{2}$ lb mince   (250 Gramm Hackfleisch)

4 trout   (4 Forellen)

1 red cabbage   (ein Rotkohl)

3 lb potatoes   (drei Pfund Kartoffel)

$\frac{1}{4}$ lb potato salad   (125 Gramm Kartoffelsalat)

$\frac{1}{2}$ lb butter   (250 Gramm Butter)

$\frac{1}{4}$ lb tea   (125 Gramm Tee)

1 lb sugar   (ein Pfund Zucker)

1 lb grey bread   (500 Gramm Graubrot)

4 pieces of strawberry flan   (4 Stück Erdbeertorte)

1 tube of ointment   (eine Tube Salbe)

1 roll of toilet paper   (eine Rolle Toilettenpapier)

1 coffee pot   (eine Kaffeekanne)

1 tin of pipe tobacco   (eine Dose Pfeifentabak)

B. What can you buy at the market? Is it open every day?

C. Where else can you buy almost everything, every day?

D. Where can you shop in the lunch hour?

5. Administration

A. Find out about the local council elections in your area, and see what differences there are compared with Ritzenburg.

B. What is the difference between a Stadtkreis and a Kreisstadt?

C. Copy the Meldeschein and fill it in (your teacher may be able to xerox it).

D. Where would you go: (i) to have a chest X-ray? (ii) to find out about jobs? (iii) to complain if you think you have paid too much tax? (iv) to have your car tested?

E. What differences do you notice between the Schupo in the picture and a British policeman?

F. Your dog has run into the road and caused a car to crash, resulting in DM 500 worth of damage. Describe what happens then.

6. Transport

A. Which way does the through traffic go? Does it go through the old part of the town? What sort of road is it and how fast can you go? And why is it difficult to find a route for a bypass? Suggest an answer to the problem.

B. You are arriving in Ritzenburg (a) by car and (b) by train. Describe your arrival.

C. What are the advantages of trams? Would it be a good idea if they had them in your town?

D. Describe a tram ride in the rush hour.

E. In what way are German buses different from those in your area?

F. If you are also studying life in France, find out the French equivalent of the Verkehrsamt. In what is it different?

G. How many different types of petrol are there? Are there more or fewer than in Britain? Where is it more expensive?

H. Why is the man in the picture worried about his new car? What sort of new car would you like? Why?

7. Schools

A. Which of the schools in Ritzenburg is most like your school? And which one would you like to go to? Why? How is it different from your school?

B. What kinds of excursion do the pupils go on?

C. What colour are the satchels worn by the children in the photo? Why?

D. What happens in the afternoon?

E. Do German pupils spend most of their time at school with the same classmates? Why?

8. Recreation and sport

A. Where would you go in your spare time in Ritzenburg if you wanted some exercise, and what would you do?

B. Compare the Ritzenburger Kickers FC with your local football club.

C. Is the Ritzenburger Turnverein only for gymnasts?

D. What happens at the Schützenfest?

E. What activities would you do to fill up the Trimmspirale?

9. Entertainment and Culture

A. What sort of thing would you like to see at the theatre? Where would you sit?

B. Find out what the seats cost at a theatre in your area and compare the prices with those at the Ritzenburg Theatre (your teacher will tell you the exchange rate, or you can ask at a bank or look it up in a paper).

C. Do the same with the cinema prices.

D. Where could you go to dance? Would you be able to stay as long as you liked? When would you leave?

E. What are the differences between your local library and the one in Ritzenburg?

F. What would you find most interesting in the museum? Why? Is there anything similar in your area?

10. Eating, Drinking and Sleeping

A. Why is the Nachmittagskaffee described as ceremonial?

B. Where do (a) the middle-aged women, (b) the young people and (c) the men go to meet their friends? And where would you go?

C. How do you get your beer in the Roter Adler? Do you fetch it yourself at the bar?

D. Point out some differences between the Gasthaus and a British pub (the beer, for a start!)

E. Choose what you would like to eat from the menu and work out how much it would cost – not forgetting VAT and service charges!

F. Collect as many names of German wines as you can from wine bottles in shops, advertisements and any likely literature your teacher may have and make a map to show where they come from.

G. Where would you sleep if you went to stay in Ritzenburg? Describe your first night there. What form do you have to fill in?

11. Three Public Services

A. What differences do you notice between refuse collection in Germany and where you live?

B. What do you think of the voluntary fire brigade in Ritzenburg? Is it a good idea?

C. Are there foreign doctors at your local hospital? Where do they come from?

D. What are the differences between the British National Health Scheme and the German Krankenkasse system?

12. Das Postamt

A. Write down what is different about German letter boxes, stamp machines and phone boxes.

B. Think of one good reason for the employee having all the money and stamps in front of him and not on the counter.

C. Start a collection of West German stamps. Whose head is shown on the ordinary ones?

13. Die Bank

A. Who pays out the money? Is it the same person who takes the request for payment?

B. Note some other things which are different from a bank in your home town.

C. Where do you go to get money to buy a house? Can *anyone* get money from them to buy *any* house? What does one have to do?

14. Die Zeitung

A. What do you find in the Ritzenburger Rundschau which is not in your local paper?
B. Would you buy the Ritzenburg local paper if you were living there, or a national daily? Give your reasons.
C. Write some imaginary items you might find on the page of local news.

15. Zwei Kirchen

A. Draw a map of Germany using vertical lines to mark where the majority of people are Catholic and horizontal lines for the parts where mostly Protestants live.
B. Compare the Protestant and Catholic churches and their services. What are the main differences?
C. Why does the Catholic Church give opinions about films? Is this a good idea, do you think?
D. Looking back at the rest of the book, find two ways in which the churches serve the whole people.

Acknowledgments

The great majority of the photographs in this book were taken by the author; thanks are due to the following for permission to reproduce the remainder:
Bundesbildstelle, Bonn (pages 13, 33 top right, 34, 43, 48)
Inter Nationes, Bad Godesberg (pages 44, 66)
Mrs. M. Wightman (pages 49, 56, 57, 62, 63, 65 bottom, 73)
Manfred Langer (page 16 top)
Reinhard Bienert (page 21 bottom)
Städt. Verkehrsamt Heidelberg (page 73 bottom right)
Verkehrsamt Sindelfingen (pages 46, 54, 55, 67)
The drawing on page 33 is by Roswitha Löhmer-Eigener. We are also grateful to the Deutscher Sportbund for permission to reproduce the *Trimmspirale* on page 50.